Effective Sentences
Writing for Success

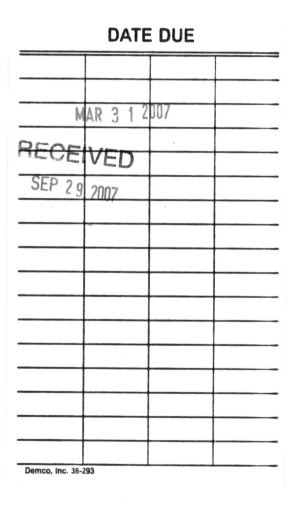

Effective Sentences
Writing for Success

Jan Fluitt-Dupuy

Ann Arbor
The University of Michigan Press

71251530

11-7-06

For my mother, Ruth Lorraine Evans Fluitt,
and for my father, Darrell Wayne Fluitt

Copyright © by the University of Michigan 2006
All rights reserved
ISBN 0-472-03146-5
(978-0-472-03146-7)
Published in the United States of America
The University of Michigan Press
Manufactured in the United States of America

∞ Printed on acid-free paper

2009   2008   2007   2006   4   3   2   1

Acknowledgments

Grateful acknowledgment is made to the following authors, publishers, and individuals for permission to reprint previously published materials.

Ben Colman for photo of the family.

Corbis for photos of graduates, chef, nurse, and dentist.

Kerri Kijewski for photos of tennis player, peaceful place in the park, active couple, and international student.

Kreutz Photography for a photo of Lance Armstrong from the 2005 Tour de France.

The following students are thanked for allowing their writing to appear in this book: Hamida Aboumador, Young Kim, Shahzad Arain, Luke Fiedorowicz, Frank Forke, Mai Nguyen, Ana Oprisan, Eleomarques Ferreira Rocha, Benito Sanchez, Martin Urbach, Endy Widjaja, Mesaynish Wodajo, and Yixin Young-Yang.

Every effort has been made to contact the copyright holders for permission to reprint borrowed material. We regret any oversights that may have occurred and will rectify them in future printings of this book.

Contents

To the Student   xi
Introduction: To the Teacher   xiii

Chapter 1: Telling about You   1
Read about Benito, Ana, and Frank

    Sentence Basics   2

    Reading and Vocabulary Activities   3
        Building Vocabulary   3
        Questions   5
        Statement Word Order   5
        Question Word Order   5

    Grammar Activities   8
        Subjects: Nouns and Pronouns   8
        Verbs: *Be* and *Have*   9
        Regular Verbs in the Simple Present Tense   10
        Fragments   11

    Writing Activities   12
        Journal Writing   12
        Transition Words   15
        Revision   15
        Editing   17

Chapter 2: Telling about a Place   18
Read about Young, Eleomarques, and Mesay

    Expanding Sentences   19
        Independent Clauses   19
        Compound Structures: Expanding Subjects and Verbs with *And*   20

    Reading Activities   21
        Building Vocabulary   21

    Grammar Activities   24
        Singular and Plural Subjects   24
        Subject-Verb Agreement   25
        There + *Be* Sentences   26
        Objects   26
        Object Pronouns   27
        Expanding Objects with *And*   27

Writing Activities   28
    Linking Sentences in Paragraphs   31
    Revision   32
    Editing   33

Chapter 3: Telling about Likes and Dislikes   34

Read about Luke, Frank, and Ana

Expanding Sentences   35
    Compound Sentences: Linking with *And, But, Or,* and *So*   35

Reading Activities   38
    Building Vocabulary   38

Grammar Activities   40
    Negatives   40
    Adjectives and Complements   42

Writing Activities   43
    Using Transition Words *First, Next, Then,* and *Finally*   47
    Revision   48
    Editing   49

Chapter 4: Telling about Family   50

Read about Endy, Martin, Mai, and Mesay

Expanding Sentences   51
    Independent and Dependent Clauses   51
    Fragments   52

Reading Activities   53
    Building Vocabulary   53

Grammar Activities   58
    Past Tense   58
    Irregular Verbs   58
    Negatives in Past Tense *Was* and *Were*   59
    Negatives in Past Tense Verbs   60
    Forming Questions with Past Tense Verbs   60
    Talking about Age in Writing   61

Writing Activities   61
    Deciding on Tense in Paragraphs and Sentences   64
    Revision   65
    Editing   66

Chapter 5: Telling about an Event   67

Read about Ibrahim, Yixin, Benito, and Ana

Expanding Sentences   68
   Complex Sentences with *Because* and *Even Though*   68

Reading Activities   70
   Building Vocabulary   70

Grammar Activities   73
   Progressive Tenses   73
   Using Quotations or *Said That*   75
   Expanding Subjects and Objects with Prepositional Phrases   76

Writing Activities   78
   Topic Sentences in Paragraphs   80
   Revision   81
   Editing   82

Chapter 6: Telling about Heroes   83

Read about Mesay, Benito, and Eleomarques

Expanding Sentences   84
   Complex Sentences with *Think, Believe,* and *Know*   84

Reading Activities   85
   Building Vocabulary   85

Grammar Activities   87
   Verb + V*ing* Forms and Verb + *To* + Verb   87
   Renaming Phrases   88

Writing Activities   90
   Writing Concluding Sentences   92
   Revision   93
   Editing   94

Chapter 7: Telling about the Future and Getting Older   95

Read about Young, Mai, Martin, and Shahzad

Expanding Sentences   96
   Complex Sentences with *That, Who,* and *Which*   96

Reading Activities   98
   Building Vocabulary   98

Grammar Activities   102
   Using the Verbs *Can* and *Could*   102
   Using the Verbs *Hope* and *Would Like*   102

Writing Activities   103
        Adding Supporting Details   106
        Revision   108
        Editing   109

Chapter 8: Telling about Future Work   110
Read about Shahzad, Ibrahim, Frank, and Endy

Expanding Sentences   111
        Compound-Complex Sentences   111

Reading Activities   113
        Building Vocabulary   113

Grammar Activities   116
        Future: Using *Will* + V   116
        Future: Using *Be Going To* + V   117

Writing Activities   118
        Sentence Variety   121
        Revision   122
        Editing   123

Appendix A: Glossary of Basic Grammar Terms   124
Appendix B: Punctuation Rules   126
Appendix C: Spelling Rules   127
Appendix D: Count and Noncount Nouns   129
Appendix E: Articles   130
Appendix F: Verb Tense Summary   131
Appendix G: Irregular Verbs   132
Appendix H: Sentence Type Summary   134

Answer Key   136

To the Student

Dear Student:

Please let me introduce you to 13 of my students. You will read their stories in this textbook. The students are listed in the order their stories appear:

- **Benito Sanchez** is from Venezuela. He is married with two children. He studies business administration.

- **Ana Oprisan** is from Romania. She is also married with two children. She studies physics.

- **Frank Forke** comes from Germany. He is in the United States to study classical guitar. He also plays Latin and flamenco music.

- **Mesaynish Wodajo** emigrated to the United States as a young girl with her family. She comes from Ethiopia. She wants to be a pharmacist.

- **Young Kim** comes from South Korea. She is married with two children. She works in an office.

- **Eleomarques Ferreira Rocha** is from Brazil. He likes to be called Leo. He wants to be an English teacher back in Brazil one day.

- **Luke Fiedorowicz** is from Poland. He came to the U.S. to study psychology.

- **Endy Widjaja** comes from Indonesia. He lives with an uncle in the U.S. He wants to work in hotel management.

- **Martin Urbach** is from Bolivia. He is a drummer. He hopes to live in the U.S. and work as a professional musician.

- **Mai Nguyen** was born in the U.S. Her parents emigrated to the U.S. in 1975. She works as a hairstylist.

- **Ibrahim Aboumador** was also born in the U.S. His parents emigrated to the U.S. from Egypt. He has finished high school. He is helping with the family business, a used car lot.

- **Yixin Young** comes from China. She is married to a Chinese-American and wants to improve her English. She worked as an accountant in China.

- **Shahzad Arain** emigrated to the U.S. from Pakistan. He lives with his parents. He studies computer science.

They are interesting people. Like you, they are working hard to improve their English. Enjoy their stories. I hope they give you good ideas for your own writing.

Sincerely,
Jan Fluitt-Dupuy

Introduction: To the Teacher

Students are the soul of this book, in real and metaphorical ways. I interviewed 13 of my former students about the eight topics that make up the chapters of this book. I wrote the readings and sentences in these chapters based on their answers. Thus, the stories you read are edited but real and authentic.

Metaphorically, these 13 students and the hundreds I have taught over the last 20 years were all before me as I wrote each page. I also thought as I wrote about those students to come—mine and yours.

Effective Sentences: Writing for Success targets high-beginning/low-intermediate students with limited English proficiency. These students, both the traditional ESOL students and Generation 1.5ers, come to our classrooms as complex, thinking beings. While these students may write English at a basic level and need our help to produce accurate sentences, they need and want to write with a complexity to match their thoughts. This text strives to answer both concerns.

Effective Sentences works with a two-part structure: (1) students first learn to recognize basic sentence structure and closely examine the basic elements to take the mystery out of the English sentence; and (2) then, students will learn about the structures that build on the basic elements to expand sentences—progressing from elements within simple sentences such as adjectives, objects, and prepositional phrases to compound and complex sentence structures.

The grammar presented here is driven by students' needs—and the stories within each chapter. The sequence of grammar is somewhat traditional—simple present tense is presented first, along with subjects and verbs, then past tense, then future—though some of the more complicated grammar points may come surprisingly early. For example, compound and complex sentence structure is introduced in Chapters 3 and 4. Even beginning students come to us using these structures, however incorrectly. In this book, grammar is simple and straightforward but never watered down. Compound structures are limited to sentences linked with *and, so,* and *but,* and complex sentences are limited to sentences with *after, before, when, while,* and *because.*

Students are free to concentrate on basic sentence building. Grammar is taught only when it is needed and is presented in an unencumbered manner. Vocabulary is open-ended. The vocabulary presented in each chapter highlights words in the readings that students may find difficult. *This is the vocabulary that students use and need:* words perhaps not on the high-frequency word lists, but pertinent to their lives nonetheless. These more difficult words are defined in the text, either through exercises or glossaries. Teachers may choose to work on these suggested vocabulary items or the vocabulary that appears in their own students' writing, either in the journals or the paragraph that each chapter culminates in. The readings themselves exist to inspire, suggest ideas, and model good writing to the students. They can be used as much or as little as teachers wish.

Paragraph structure is introduced from Chapter 1 because sentences, after all, do not exist in isolation and are always within context. Therefore, some paragraph structure is mentioned at various points in the text. For example, transitions come in Chapter 1 because even simple sentences need some sort of linking in paragraphs. Even at this early point, *however, then*, and *also* are introduced as cohesive devices. In later chapters, students learn about topic sentences, general-to-specific movement, and sentence variety within paragraph structure.

It is important to work through the chapters of this text in order because earlier chapters lay a foundation for later ones. As I interviewed students and asked questions about the topics in this book—their families, favorite places, major events, and so forth—I simply wrote down their answers without editing. Later, as I crafted their stories in clear and simple prose, I thought carefully about the grammatical structures they needed to communicate this vital information about their lives. I had to balance the level of complexity of their stories with the traditional sequence of grammar.

Some topics—*family* is just one example—had to come later in the grammatical sequence. Discussing family means discussing past events—when family members moved, were married, were born. Telling about families requires numbers for dates of significant events and ages and comparative adjectives to describe sibling order. These grammatical structures should be taught after more basic topics like subjects, verbs, objects, and present tense are explored. The last chapters deal with the most complex issues for beginning writers: noun clauses, adjective clauses, and future time. It is appropriate to reference these topics toward the end of the book.

I hope you enjoy using this text as much as I have enjoyed writing it. It has been rewarding for me to sit with my students in the quiet of my study and spin their stories for others to continue the web of learning.

1 Telling about You

Who are you? When you meet people for the first time, what do you say about yourself?

In this chapter, you will:

↪ read about three students: Benito, Ana, and Frank.

↪ write sentences about yourself and others.

↪ learn about subjects and verbs.

↪ learn about the process of writing.

Sentence Basics

What do sentences in English look like? A simple sentence has four important parts:

1. a capital letter at the beginning.
2. a period (.), question mark (?), or an exclamation point (!) at the end.
3. a subject that tells who or what the sentence is about.
4. a verb that tells about the action of the sentence.

A simple sentence has just one **subject** and one **verb.**

Examples: S = Subject V = Verb

     S + V

Benito works hard.

     S   +   V

The apartment is small.

Activity 1. Discovering Sentence Basics

Some simple sentences follow. Examine each closely for these four parts:

- a capital letter
- a period, question mark, or exclamation point
- a subject
- a verb

With a partner, try to find the main parts of the sentence.

- Put a number 1 above the capital letters at the beginning of each sentence.
- Put a number 2 above the period, question mark, or exclamation point.
- Circle the subject of each sentence.
- Underline the verb of each sentence.

The first is done for you.

Example:

  1   2

(I) am from Nicaragua.

1
2

1. (I) am a student.

2. My name is Ana.

3. Does she study hard?

4. Don't touch that!

5. Where do the students live?

6. Frank walks to class every day.

7. They eat together every night.

8. You look so pretty!

9. Is her son 16 years old already?

10. Her husband works at the university too.

Reading and Vocabulary Activities

Building Vocabulary

To speak and write in English, you need words. Learning new words in English (or any language) is building vocabulary. Don't worry. You know a lot of English words already.

These exercises will help you remember more words. You will also share your words with a partner and a group so that you can learn new ones.

Activity 2. Thinking about Vocabulary

Working with a partner, think and talk about the answers to the questions. Write your answers in the blanks.

1. What do you say when you meet someone for the first time? Think of at least one or two questions.

_____

_____

_____

2. Now think of one or two more questions. What topics do you discuss with someone you do not know well?

_____

_____

_____

As a class, put some of these sentences on the board. Your teacher will help you with the correct grammar. When you are sure the grammar is correct, copy the sentences on the blanks:

_____

_____

_____

_____

_____

_____

Activity 3. Read and Respond

Read the short dialogues, silently at first, and then practice speaking the sentences aloud. Compare these sentences with those you wrote in Activity 2.

Dialogue 1
Question: What is your name?
Answer: My name is Benito.
Question: What do you do?
Answer: I am a student in business administration.

Dialogue 2
Question: Hi. What is your name?
Answer: My name is Ana.
Question: Where do you come from?
Answer: I am from a small town in Romania.

Dialogue 3
Question: Hello. What is your name?
Answer: My name is Frank.
Question: Where are you from?
Answer: I am from Germany.
Question: Do you like living here?
Answer: Yes, I like it very much.

Questions

In Activities 2 and 3 you were asked to read and write questions that people ask when they are meeting someone for the first time. As we have seen, questions are one type of sentence. Questions have a different word order.

Activity 4. Word Order

Look closely at the three types of sentences that follow. What differences do you see? (Hint—look at subjects and verbs!)

Examples: I am from Romania.

Do you like living in this country?

I like it very much!

What differences did you notice? Write them on the blanks.

_____

_____

_____

Statement Word Order

Statements and most exclamations use this word order:

S + V

Examples:

S   V
I study hard.

S   V
Frank loves Latin American music!

Question Word Order

Questions use a different word order from statements. In questions, the subject and verb change places. Where is the verb in these examples?

Is your name Benito?

Are you from Romania?

What is your name?

Where are you from?

Some questions use a *do* verb. *Do* is a **helping verb** and comes before the subject. Look at these examples:

> Does she study hard?
>
> Do you go to school?
>
> What do you study?
>
> Where do you go to school?

Activity 5. Fill-in-the-Blank

Fill in the blanks with the words given in parentheses. Pay attention to the proper word order for questions and statements. The words given in the parentheses may be mixed up! The first one is done for you.

1. (is, name)

   What ___is___ your ___name___ ?

2. (is, name)

   My _____ _____ Benito.

3. (do, you)

   What _____ _____ do?

4. (are, you)

   _____ _____ a student?

5. (am, I)

   Yes, _____ _____ a student in business administration.

6. (she, does)

   Where _____ _____ come from?

7. (she, is)

   _____ _____ from a small town in Romania.

8. (they, do)

   _____ _____ like living here?

9. (like, they)

   Yes, _____ _____ it very much.

10. (they, do)

    Why _____ _____ like it so much?

Activity 6. Read

Read the paragraph two or three times. Read once for a basic understanding. Then underline any words you do not understand. Use a dictionary to look up any words you don't understand. Read again for a full understanding.

Benito is a student at City University. He is from Venezuela. He studies business administration. He lives on campus in an apartment. He thinks the apartment is small. However, he likes being near his classes. Benito also likes his classes. He likes the professors at the university. They are very helpful to their students.

Activity 7. Respond

Answer the questions about the reading. Use complete sentences. Use S + V word order. The first one is done for you.

1. What does Benito do?   <u>Benito is a student at City University.</u>

   _____

2. Where is he from? _____

   _____

3. What does he study? _____

   _____

4. Where does he live? _____

   _____

5. What does he think about his apartment? _____

   _____

6. What does he like about his apartment? _____

   _____

7. What does he like about the university? _____

   _____

8. Why does he like about his professors? _____

   _____

Grammar Activities

Subjects: Nouns and Pronouns

Subjects are nouns in the first part of sentences. There are two types of nouns.

Common nouns are general words for people, places, things, or feelings. Some examples of common nouns are *student, apartment, classes,* and *love.*

Proper nouns are names of specific people or places like *Benito, Ana,* and *Venezuela.* Pronouns can be subjects too. Pronouns take the place of nouns.

The **subject pronouns** in English are

Singular (one)	Plural (more than one)
I	*we*
you	*you*
he/she/it	*they*

Activity 8. Changing Nouns to Pronouns

Practice using subject pronouns. Change the subjects (in bold) to pronouns. Write the complete sentence. The first one is done for you.

1. **Ana** is married.

   <u>She is married.</u>

2. **Ana** studies physics.

   _____

3. Does **her husband** study physics too?

   _____

4. **Ana and her husband** have two children!

   _____

5. **Ana and I** are good friends.

   _____

6. **Frank** studies music.

   _____

7. Does **City University** have a good music program?

   _____

8. **Frank and his brother** are from a small town in Germany.

   _____

9. **A small town** is a peaceful place to live.

   _____

10. **Big cities** can be exciting places to live.

   _____

Verbs: *Be* and *Have*

Verbs show action or being. **Action verbs** tell what the subject is doing in the sentence. *Be* **verbs** tell about the subject. Verbs also have tense. The **tense** of the verb tells about the time.

The Verbs *to be* and *to have* in the Simple Present Tense

Memorize these very common verbs. They are **irregular verbs.**

	Singular	Plural
to be	*I am*	*We are*
	You are	*You are*
	He/she/it is	*They are*
to have	*I have*	*We have*
	You have	*You have*
	He/She/It has	*They have*

Activity 9. Using *Be* and *Have*

Use the correct form of the verb to be *in the sentences. The first one is done for you.*

1. We _____*are*_____ new in this city.

2. You _____ 25 years old.

3. I _____ a musician.

4. Frank _____ a good student.

5. Benito and his wife _____ from Venezuela.

Now, use the correct form of the verb to have.

6. His wife _____ a long walk to school.

7. I _____ so much work to do!

8. You _____ a car.

9. Benito _____ two children.

10. We _____ a nice dorm room.

Regular Verbs in the Simple Present Tense

A simple present tense verb is just one word. For most of the subject pronouns (*I, we, you, they*), the **simple present tense** verb form is the base form of the verb. The base form is part of the verb found in the dictionary:

	Singular	Plural
to work	*I work* *You work*	*We work* *You work* *They work*

Third person singular pronouns have an *–s* added to the base form:

He / She / It **works.**

Activity 10. Using the Simple Present Tense

Fill in the blanks with the correct form of the verbs in parentheses.

1. Americans _____drive_____ *(drive)* everywhere!

2. I _____ *(walk)* to work.

3. You _____ *(live)* very close to the university.

4. Ana _____ *(work)* as a physics teacher.

5. Benito and I _____ *(like)* spicy foods.

6. Frank _____ *(learn)* very quickly.

7. His wife _____ *(come)* from a big city.

8. I _____ *(hate)* my apartment.

9. Frank and his roommate _____ *(study)* together every night.

10. The dog _____ *(enjoy)* long walks.

Fragments

All sentences need a subject and a verb. If either is missing, the group of words is not complete and is not a sentence. It is a fragment, and it is a serious mistake.

Examples:

S + V = sentence
She <u>lives</u> in an apartment.

S only = fragment
She   in an apartment.

V only = fragment
Lives in an apartment.

Activity 11. Finding Fragments

Look for subjects and verbs in the sentences that follow. If either a subject or verb is missing, the sentence is a fragment. Write the letter F in the blank of each fragment. Then correct the sentence by adding either a subject or a verb. If the sentence is correct, write the letter S in the blank. The first two are done for you.

<u>S</u> 1. Ana has two children.

  <u>   correct (no change)   </u>

<u>F</u> 2. The children teenagers.

  <u>   The children are teenagers.   </u>

____ 3. Live with their parents in an apartment near the university.

  <u>   </u>

____ 4. They go to a U.S. high school.

  <u>   </u>

____ 5. The oldest child, Andraei, likes computer science.

  <u>   </u>

____ 6. The youngest one, Andra, art and literature.

_____

____ 7. They good in mathematics.

_____

____ 8. They good grades in school.

_____

____ 9. Ana and her husband want them to go to good universities in the U.S.

_____

____ 10. The children study hard even in summer.

_____

Writing Activities

Journal Writing

Many successful writers get ideas for writing by keeping a journal. A journal is a notebook where a writer can write ideas down quickly without worrying about making mistakes. No one needs to see your journal. The sentences you write in your journal can be used for other writing assignments.

Your journal should be separate from your other writing. Use a notebook or write on loose-leaf sheets in a three-ring binder.

Write in your journal often. Try to write a little, such as four or five sentences, every day at the same time of day, five to seven times a week. Write down any thoughts or questions quickly. Once you have started writing, try to keep on writing. See if you can fill a page with sentences! Don't worry about grammar. You can correct the sentences later if you decide to use them in a paragraph.

Activity 12. Journal Topics

Are you ready to write just for fun? Write for 15 minutes without stopping on one of these topics. Try a new topic each day.

1. Write about your school. What do you study? Where do you study? Do you like it?

2. Write about where you live. Is it an apartment or a house? Do you like it? What are the good things about living there?

3. Write about what your average day is like. What part of your day do you find boring? What part do you find exciting?

4. Write about your favorite animals. What kinds of animals do you like? Do you have any pets?

Activity 13. Guided Sentence Practice

Answer the questions in full sentences. Start with a capital letter and end with a period or an exclamation point. Check for subjects and verbs.

1. What is your name?

   _____

2. How old are you?

   _____

3. Where are you from?

   _____

4. Are you a student?

   _____

5. What do you study?

   _____

6. Do you have a job?

   _____

7. What work do you do?

   _____

8. Where do you live?

_____

9. Do you like living in the U.S.?

_____

10. What do you like about living here?

_____

11. What do you miss most from your country?

_____

Activity 14. Writing a First Draft

On a separate page, write a paragraph introducing yourself. Write about ten sentences. Use the sentences you wrote in Activities 12 and 13, and add more sentences if you like. Reread Benito's paragraph (see Activity 6 on page 7). Frank's and Ana's paragraphs follow. You may get some ideas from their writing too.

Sample Paragraphs:

A Little Bit about Me
by Frank Forke

I am Frank Forke. I am from a small town in Germany, Lilletaal. It is twelve kilometers outside of the larger city of Bremen. I like the peacefulness and slow pace of a small town. However, I also enjoy the excitement of a big city. I am a musician. I play the guitar. I especially love Spanish and Latin American music. I want to earn a degree in music from City University. Then, I want to teach music and play as a professional.

An Introduction
by Ana Oprisan

My name is Ana. I am from Romania. I teach physics. I also study physics at City University. I am married. My husband studies at the university too. We have two children. Our son's name is Andraei. He is sixteen years old. Our daughter's name is Andra. She is fourteen. We live in a small apartment near the university.

Transition Words

When writers link sentences in a paragraph, they sometimes add words to make the ideas between the sentences more clear. These words are often adverbs. **Adverbs** are words that add meaning to verbs, adjectives, sentences, or other adverbs. Adverbs that link sentences are called **transitions.** Look at the examples from Benito's, Ana's, and Frank's paragraphs:

- He thinks the apartment is small. **However,** he likes being near his classes.
- I like the peacefulness and slow pace of a small town. **However,** I also enjoy the excitement of a big city.
- I want to earn a degree in music from City University. **Then,** I want to teach music and play as a professional.
- My husband studies at the university **too.**

Transitions often come at the beginning of the sentences but not always. Try using transitions in your paragraphs.

Revision

Even good writers do not write a perfect paragraph the first time. They write first, and then they rewrite. They look back over what they have written and make decisions. They can add or take away what does not seem to fit. This process is called **revision.**

Revision is hard work. It is difficult to see how a paragraph can be changed to make it better. Other readers can help. Your classmates will help you revise your paragraph.

Activity 15. Peer Editing

Show your paragraph to two or three classmates. Ask them to answer the questions on the form. Your teacher will also read your paragraph.

Reader's Name _____

Writer's Name _____

1. Is there any place where you want more information? Are there any sentences that are confusing? Write these sentences. Suggest changes, if possible.

   _____

   _____

   _____

   _____

   _____

2. Are there any sentences that use transitions? Write them. Which sentences could use transitions?

   _____

   _____

   _____

   _____

   _____

3. What is the best thing about this paragraph? What does the writer do well?

   _____

   _____

   _____

   _____

   _____

Activity 16. Writing Additional Drafts

Write a second draft of your paragraph on a separate sheet of paper. Use the ideas of your classmates and your teacher to write a better paragraph.

✔ Editing

When you are sure all the information in your paragraph is there, it is time to check grammar. Looking for grammatical mistakes is called editing. **Editing** can be even harder than revision. It is often difficult to see mistakes in your own work. However, you must learn to find and correct most, if not all, of your mistakes.

Try looking for only one type of mistake at a time. Look only at parts of sentences. Don't just read over the paragraph. It is easier to check just one part at a time.

Activity 17. Working on Grammar

Look for mistakes in your paragraph. Check parts of sentences in this order:

- Look at **subjects** first. Make sure that plural subjects have -*s* endings or are plural subject pronouns. Make sure that singular subjects do not have an -*s* ending.

- Look at the **verbs,** especially the verbs with third person singular subjects, *he, she,* or *it.* Are they in present tense? Those verbs should have an -*s* ending.

- Do you have both **a subject and a verb** in each sentence? Fix any fragments that you find.

- Are there places where a **transition** word like *however, then,* or *also* might help your paragraph?

Activity 18. Preparing a Final Draft

When you feel sure that the grammar is as good as you can make it, hand in this last draft to your teacher. He or she may find more words that need to be changed. Make these changes. Then hand in a final draft.

2 Telling about a Place

What is your favorite place? Where do you like to go when you can? What place do you dream about? Does this special place make your day brighter?

In this chapter, you will:

🐾 read about three students: Young, Eleomarques, and Mesay.

🐾 begin a vocabulary notebook.

🐾 learn about compound structures.

🐾 read and write about special places.

Expanding Sentences

Independent Clauses

In Chapter 1, you learned about simple sentences. You learned that a simple sentence has one subject and one verb. The test for a sentence is to ask a question, **Who** or **what** is **doing what action?** The word that answers the **who-or-what** question is the **subject.** The word that answers the **what-action** question is the **verb.** Look at this example:

    S   V
Benito walks to school every day.

Who is doing what action?

Benito = Subject   *walks* = Verb

Some sentences with a *be* verb or another linking verb have no real action. The test question is a little different: *Who or what is being described?* Look at this example:

    S   V
Mesay is happy in her new home.

Who is being described?

Mesay = Subject   *is* = Verb

There are usually many other words besides the subject and verb of a simple sentence—other nouns and pronouns, adjectives, adverbs, phrases, and clauses. These other words are there because they add more information. You will learn more about these words later. For now pay attention to finding the subject and verb of each sentence.

Simple sentences present complete thoughts and make sense. They can stand alone and still have meaning. Simple sentences are also called **independent clauses** because they can stand alone. They are independent. A **clause** is a group of words that contains a subject and a verb.

Activity 1. Testing for Independent Clauses

Answer the question **who** *(or* **what***) is doing what action?* *to find the subject and verb of each independent clause. For* be *verbs answer the question* **who** *(or* **what***) is being described?* *The first one is done for you.*

1. Young is from South Korea. **Who is being described?**

    Subject _____Young_____   Verb _____is_____

2. She misses her city very much. **Who is doing what action?**

    Subject _____   Verb _____

3. Beautiful mountains are close to her city. **What is being described?**

    Subject _____   Verb _____

4. The people come to see the mountains. **Who is doing what action?**

    Subject _____   Verb _____

5. Many people ski there in the winter. **Who is doing what action?**

    Subject _____   Verb _____

Compound Structures: Expanding Subjects and Verbs with *And*

We can add information to simple sentences by expanding the subject and verb. We can add two or more subjects separated by the word **and.** Verbs can be expanded in the same way.

S
Benito walks to school every day.

S + *and* + S
Benito and Irma walk to school every day.

S   + S + *and* +   S
Benito, Irma, and their children walk to school every day.

       V
Mesay *is* happy in her new home.

       V   +   *and* + V
Mesay *is* happy in her new home *and likes* the neighborhood too.

Activity 2. Making Compound Subjects and Verbs

Make the subjects and verbs compound by adding and *plus the word in parentheses. Some of the sentences will have both compound subjects and compound verbs. The first one is done for you.*

1. Salvador (Recife) are cities in Brazil.

    _____Salvador and Recife are cities in Brazil._____

2. Leo (his family) live in Salvador.

    _____

3. Two million people live (work) in Salvador.

    _____

4. Many traditions (customs) come from West African slaves.

    _____

5. Brazilian food (music) are popular with the visitors.

    _____

6. Millions of people sing (dance) in the streets during Carnival.

    _____

 # Reading Activities

Building Vocabulary

It is important for you to learn many new words in English. A vocabulary notebook is a good way to do this. This notebook can be any size. It can be small enough to fit into a pocket or purse. It can be large enough to keep on your desk or beside your bed. This notebook must be easy for you to use. You should look at it many times a day.

During the day make note of any new words you see and hear. Look for new words in the newspaper or on television. Look at signs around town. Listen for new words as teachers and friends talk. Write these down on a piece of paper or in your notebook. When you sit down to study each day, take the time to look them up in the dictionary. Find out what the word means in your native language. But also look at other dictionaries. Write the meaning (in English) and the part of speech (noun, verb, adjective, adverb, or preposition) in your notebook. If the dictionary gives a sample sentence, write that as well.

Study these words as often as you can. Look at the list at least once a day, or more. Soon these new words will be easy for you. Try to use one or two of your new words each day. You will be surprised at how fast you can build up your word power.

Activity 3. Starting a Vocabulary Notebook

Use this model to start your notebook.

Word	Part of Speech	Meaning	Sample Sentence
vocabulary	noun	all the words that exist in a particular language or subject	Reading helps to improve your vocabulary.
tradition	noun	a way of acting for a group of people for a long time	Our traditions come from West Africa.

Activity 4. Reading

Read the paragraph two or three times. Read once for a basic understanding. Then underline any words you do not understand. Use a dictionary to look up these words. Read again for a full understanding.

My Favorite Place on Earth
by Young Kim

My favorite place on earth is my hometown, Gangreung. It is on the east coast of South Korea. Mountains, lakes, and the ocean are all nearby. There is plenty of natural beauty and no pollution. Many tourists visit there. They find friendly people and good seafood. Winters are not too cold. Visitors come and stay during all four seasons. In the spring they hike in the mountains. They go to the beach in the summer. In the fall they go to see the lovely changing leaves. There is skiing in the winter. I miss my hometown. I hope to live there again one day.

Activity 5. Respond

Answer the questions about the reading. Use complete sentences. The first one is done for you.

1. What is Young's favorite place on earth? <u>Young's favorite place on earth</u>

    <u>is her hometown, Gangreung.</u> _____

2. Where is Gangreung? _____

    _____

3. What is nearby? _____

    _____

4. What do tourists find there? _____

    _____

5. What are the winters like? _____

    _____

6. What do tourists do in the spring? In the summer? In the fall? In the winter? _____

    _____

    _____

    _____

7. How does Young feel about Gangreung? _____

    _____

8. What does Young hope for? _____

    _____

Activity 6. Recognizing Compound Structures

*In the reading, Young uses compound structures. Highlight the parts of sentences linked by **and**. Notice the sentences that begin with* there is. *You will study this sentence pattern later in this chapter. Write the two sentences with expanded subjects and verbs.*

1. Copy here Young's sentence with three subjects: _____

   _____

2. Copy here Young's sentence with two verbs: _____

   _____

Grammar Activities

Singular and Plural Subjects

As you already know, subjects are nouns. Nouns can be **singular** (only one) or **plural** (more than one). When subjects are expanded by adding *and* between two or more nouns, the verb must be plural too.

Benito walks to school every day.

Benito = one person   *walks* = singular

Benito, Irma, and their children walk to school every day.

Benito, Irma, and their children = 4 persons   *walk* = plural

Note the use of commas with compound structures. If there are more than three words in the list, add a comma after each word before the *and*. If there are just two words linked by *and,* a comma is not needed.

Activity 7. Identifying Singular and Plural Subjects

*Read the sentences, and circle the subjects. Write **S** above singular subjects and **P** above plural subjects. Underline the verb in each sentence. The first one is done for you.*

       S
1. Mesay <u>is</u> a student.

2. She wants to be a pharmacist.

3. Mesay comes from Ethiopia.

4. Her name is short for Mesaynish.

5. She and her sister are in college.

6. Etsegenet is the name of her sister.

7. Mesay and Etsegenet study hard.

8. They have two little brothers.

9. Samson and Kidus are their names.

10. Mesay, Samson, and Kidus live at home with their parents.

Subject-Verb Agreement

Notice the position of the *-s* endings on nouns and verbs:

Benito **walks** to school every day.

Benito = singular   walk**s** = singular

An *-s* ending on a present tense verb means singular.

The **kids** walk to school every day.

The kid**s** = plural   walk = plural

An *-s* ending on a noun means plural. Be careful! Subjects and verbs must **agree.** That means they must match. A singular subject takes a singular verb. Plural subjects take plural verbs. In present tense, you will not have two *-s* endings. Always check subjects and verbs.

Activity 8. Making Subjects and Verbs Agree

Read the sentences, and circle the correct verb. The first one is done for you.

1. Young miss / misses her hometown.

2. Gangreung has / have a lot of natural beauty.

3. The mountains, lakes, and the ocean is / are all very beautiful.

4. Many tourists comes / come to see these places.

5. The people hikes / hike in the mountains.

There + *Be* Sentences

Here is an easy sentence pattern.

There + *is* + singular noun.

There + *are* + plural noun.

This pattern is used often in speaking and informal writing. The subject of the sentence actually *follows* the verbs. Words can be added after the subject to add information. Look at these sample sentences:

There is a good school in that city.

There are many apartments close to campus.

Remember, subjects and verbs must agree. Check the subject **after** the verb to make it singular or plural.

Activity 9. Agreement with *There* + *Be* Sentences

*Look for the subject of each sentence, and decide if it is singular or plural. Then write either **is** or **are** in the blank. The first one is done for you.*

1. There _____are_____ two million people in Salvador, Brazil.

2. There _____ a lot of visitors in my city too.

3. There _____ wonderful food to eat.

4. There _____ many types of music.

5. There _____ many traditions from West African slaves.

Objects

We have studied nouns as subjects. As subjects, nouns tell who or what is doing the action of the verb. Nouns can also be objects and follow verbs. Objects tell who or what is receiving the action of the verb. (Obj = Object)

S + V   +   Obj

Frank plays the guitar.

What does Frank play? the guitar

S + V   +   Obj

Ana studies physics.

What does Ana study? physics

Object Pronouns

In Chapter 1 you learned about subject pronouns. Pronouns can also take the place of nouns that are objects.

The **object pronouns** in English are

Singular (one)	Plural (more than one)
me	*us*
you	*you*
him/her/it	*them*

Expanding Objects with *And*

We can expand objects in the same way that we can expand subjects and verbs. You simply add *and* between the objects.

Obj   +   Obj + *and* + Obj

Frank plays *the guitar, the flute, and the drums.*

Obj + *and* Obj

Ana studies *physics* and *English.*

Activity 10. Recognizing Compound Objects

In the sample paragraph in Activity 13 on page 30, Leo uses compound objects. Read and highlight the objects linked by **and.** *Write the two sentences with expanded subjects and verbs. The first one is done for you.*

1. Copy here Leo's first sentences with compound objects: <u>Many people</u>

   <u>visit Salvador to explore this heritage and culture.</u>

2. Copy here Leo's second sentence with compound objects: _____

   _____

3. What other compound structures does Leo use? Copy those three
   sentences here: _____

   _____

   _____

For extra practice, read Mesay's sample paragraph in Activity 13, and high-light the compound structures she uses.

Writing Activities

In this chapter you will write a paragraph about a special place. This place may be your hometown, as Young and Leo write about. You may decide, however, to write about a smaller space, such as your room, a favorite park, or a building. Read Mesay's paragraph on page 30. She tells about the house she lives in with her parents.

First, let's do some writing exercises to get you thinking.

Activity 11. Journal Topics

Let's prepare for your next formal writing assignment by writing just for fun. Write for 15 minutes without stopping on one of the following topics. Try a new topic each day. Remember, grammar and mistakes are not so important. You are trying to get ideas, and you are practicing putting those ideas in written English.

1. Write about the places that you shop here. Are they easy to get to? Do you like shopping in this country? Why or why not?

2. Write about the places where you go in your free time to enjoy nature. What are they like? Describe a special place of natural beauty.

3. Write about the places you like to go to eat a special meal. What kind of food is served there? What does your special restaurant look like?

4. Write about the places you go with friends. Where are they? What do you do there? How often do you go?

Activity 12. Guided Sentence Practice

Answer the questions in full sentences. Pay attention to all parts of the sentence, particularly subjects and verbs.

1. Where do you come from? _____

   _____

2. Where is it located? _____

   _____

3. How many people live there? _____

   _____

4. What do visitors find interesting about this place? _____

   _____

5. Why do they find them interesting?_____

_____

6. Are there important traditions? Write sentences about each special
tradition. _____

_____

_____

7. What makes these traditions special?_____

_____

_____

8. How often do you get to visit? _____

_____

9. Do you hope to live there again? Why? _____

_____

Activity 13. Writing a First Draft

In the space provided or on a separate page, write a paragraph about a special place you have lived. Use the sentences you wrote in Activity 12 as a guide. You may also follow the reading sample in Activity 4 on page 22 as a guide or the sample paragraphs that follow.

_____

_____

_____

_____

_____

_____

_____

_____

_____

_____

Sample Paragraphs:

My Hometown: Salvador Brazil
by Eleomarques Ferreira Rocha

I come from a large seaside city in Brazil called Salvador. There are more than two million people in this hilly city. West African slaves came here from the 16th century. Their heritage makes our culture rich. Many people visit Salvador to explore this heritage and culture. Africa influences our food. Salvadoran cooks use peanuts, coconut, and okra to make some of our delicious dishes. Our music and dance also have roots in Africa. Capoeira is one of our traditional dances. It is actually a type of fighting. Slaves in the field would dance and fight. Many traditional instruments keep the rhythm of capoeira. Many visitors also come to Salvador for the music and dance of Carnival in the spring. My city is full of a wonderful heritage.

Our Home
by Mesaynish Wodajo

We are proud of our house in America. My father and mother worked and saved for many years to buy it. We moved in about a year ago. Guests enter our house from the front door. There is a small hallway there. To the right, there are stairs to the second story. Further to the right is the family room with a TV and our computer. To the left of the hallway is a large carpeted living room. There are two sofas there, a coffee table, a shelf of books, and a stereo. The living room leads to the dining room. We eat our special meals there. The dining room connects to the kitchen and a laundry area. My bedroom, with a bath and shower, is also downstairs, next to the family room. Upstairs there are three bedrooms and two full baths. Outside there is a garage for our car. We also have a nice yard with space for a garden. It is a nice house with plenty of sunshine and room. My family is very comfortable here.

Linking Sentences in Paragraphs

Sentences in paragraphs need to "hang together." They need to connect in some way. One way to do this is to repeat key words and phrases. Another way to do this is to use pronouns linked to nouns. Reread Leo's paragraph that follows. Note the boldfaced words. These are the linking words. They help make the paragraph understandable.

Sample Paragraph:

My Hometown: Salvador Brazil

by Eleomarques Ferreira Rocha

(1) I come from a large seaside **city** in Brazil called **Salvador.** (2) There are more than two million people in **this** hilly **city.** (3) West **African** slaves came **here** from the 16th century. (4) **Their heritage** makes our **culture** rich. (5) Many people visit **Salvador** to explore **this heritage** and **culture.** (6) **Africa** influences our food. (7) **Salvadoran** cooks use peanuts, coconut, and okra to make some of our delicious dishes. (8) Our **music and dance** also have roots in **Africa.** (9) **Capoeira** is one of our traditional **dances.** (10) **It** is actually a type of fighting. (11) **Slaves** in the field would **dance** and fight. (12) Many traditional instruments keep the rhythm of **capoeira.** (13) Many visitors also come to **Salvador** for the **music and dance** of Carnival in the spring. (14) My **city** is full of a wonderful **heritage.**

Activity 14: Finding Linking Words

Look at these key words from Leo's paragraph. Which sentences contain linking words to the key words? Look at the boldfaced words and the numbers in front of each sentence in the paragraph above. Show which sentences contain linking words. Discuss how they make the paragraph more understandable. The first is done for you.

1. city, Salvador: <u>sentences numbered 1, 2, 3, 5, 7, 13, and 14</u>

2. African slaves: _____

3. heritage and culture: _____

4. music and dance: _____

Revision

Activity 15. Peer Editing

Show your paragraph to two or three classmates. Ask them to answer the questions on the form. Your teacher will also read your paragraph.

Reader's Name _____

Writer's Name _____

1. What do you like most about the place the author is describing? Why?

   _____

   _____

   _____

   _____

2. Count the number of compound structures the author uses. Write them here:

   _____

   _____

   _____

   _____

   _____

3. Where do you need or want more information? What can be added?

   _____

   _____

   _____

4. What is the best thing about this paragraph? What does the writer do well?

   _____

   _____

   _____

   _____

Activity 16. Writing Additional Drafts

Write a second draft of your paragraph on a separate sheet of paper. Use the ideas of your classmates and your teacher to write a better paragraph.

✔ Editing

It is time to check grammar. Remember to look for only one type of error at a time. One trick is to look only at one sentence at a time. With two sheets of paper, cover all parts of your paragraph except for one individual sentence. Start from the bottom of the page. Search sentence by sentence for the following structures.

Activity 17. Working on Grammar

Look for mistakes in your paragraph. Check parts of sentences in this order:

- Check **compound structures.** Look at every *and* in your writing. Is a noun linked with another noun? Are verbs linked together? Do you link nouns as objects? If you link more than three words, are they separated by commas?
- Look at **subject-verb agreement.** Find each subject and verb and see if they "match." If there are compound subjects, make sure the verb is plural. Pay close attention to third person singular subjects and verbs.
- Add any **transition words and linking words** to connect your sentences.
- Check for any **fragments.**

Activity 18. Preparing a Final Draft

When you feel sure that the grammar is as good as you can make it, hand in this last draft to your teacher. He or she may find more words that need to be changed. Make these changes. Then hand in a final draft.

3 Telling about Likes and Dislikes

What do you like to do in your free time? What are the things that you don't like to do?

In this chapter, you will:

☝ meet a new student, Luke, and read more about Frank and Ana.

☝ learn about compound sentences.

☝ study negative verbs, adjectives, and complements.

☝ write about your own likes and dislikes.

Expanding Sentences

Compound Sentences: Linking with *And, But, Or,* and *So*

You have learned that subjects, verbs, and objects can be linked by *and*. In fact, any words, phrases, or clauses—if they are the same grammatical structures—can be linked in this way. Independent clauses are often linked by *and*. In Chapter 2 you learned that simple sentences are also called independent clauses because they can stand alone. The subject and verb in an independent clause present a complete thought and makes sense on their own. A **compound sentence** is two independent clauses linked by *and*. Here is an example of a compound sentence:

> S + V + Obj *, and*   S + V + Obj
> Frank plays the guitar, **and** his roommate plays the drums.

Note that a comma comes before the *and* when two independent clauses are linked together. That comma is an important signal that another independent clause is coming. The comma should <u>not</u> be omitted.

Compound sentences connect two important ideas. They make your writing smoother. *And* is not the only word that can link sentences. There are six others, called **coordinating conjunctions**: *but, or, so, for, yet, nor*. It can be helpful to remember these conjunctions with the word **FANBOYS**:

> **F** or
>
> **A** nd
>
> **N** or
>
> **B** ut
>
> **O** r
>
> **Y** et
>
> **S** o

The most common coordinating conjunctions are *and, but, or,* and *so*.

The word *and* carries the meaning of an additional idea as we have seen. The word *but* can also show addition but is more commonly used to express a difference from the first sentence.

<u>Example</u>: Frank plays the guitar, but he also plays the drums.

The word *or* is used to explain another possibility.

<u>Example</u>: Frank practices in the morning, or he plays late at night.

The word *so* is used to show that the second sentence is a result of the first sentence.

<u>Example</u>: Frank practices many hours a week, so he can improve quickly.

Activity 1. Combining Sentences with *And, But, Or,* and *So*

Combine the groups of sentences into one compound sentence. In the first four items, use the conjunction in parentheses. In the other items, decide which coordinating conjunction to use. The first one is done for you. Read more about Mesay's house.

1. Our house is new to us. I love it already. (but)

   Our house is new to us, but I love it already.

2. The house is in a quiet neighborhood. It is convenient to shopping and schools. (and)

   _____

   _____

3. I study in my room. I work at the computer in the den. (or)

   _____

   _____

4. The kitchen is next to the dining room. We eat most of our meals at the dining room table. (so)

   _____

   _____

5. My bedroom has a good view of the backyard. I love looking at the pretty garden.

   _____

   _____

6. We spend family time in the living room listening to music. We watch TV in the den.

   _____

   _____

7. My parents sleep in one bedroom with a door leading to a bathroom. There is another bedroom with a bathroom in it.

   _____

   _____

8. I am the oldest child. I have the other bedroom and bath.

   _____

   _____

9. My parents want to sleep close to my little brothers. They sleep in the upstairs bedroom next to their rooms.

   _____

   _____

10. I sleep downstairs next to the kitchen. I do not go in there late at night for snacks!

    _____

    _____

Activity 2. Comparing Simple and Compound Sentences

In this activity you will find simple and compound sentences. If the sentence is simple (S + V), write the letter S in the blank. If the sentence is complex (S + V + Obj + **,** *+* **conjunction** *+ S + V + Obj), write the letter C in the blank. Be careful! Remember that simple sentences can sometimes have more than one subject, verb, or object. The first two are done for you.*

___S___ 1. Young paints and draws on Saturday mornings.
Here are one subject and two verbs. The and *separates the verbs.*

___C___ 2. She is busy, but she takes the time to study art.
Here are two separate S + V structures. The but *separates the two clauses.*

_____ 3. Young works, goes to school, and takes care of her family.

_____ 4. She wants to draw and paint better, so she wants to take more lessons.

_____ 5. Shahzad loves to see new places and people.

_____ 6. He wants to travel to Yellowstone Park and the Grand Canyon.

_____ 7. He is in school now, so he is too busy to travel.

_____ 8. Yixin's father is a table tennis coach, and he is her best teacher.

_____ 9. Yixin lives far away from her father now, but he still teaches her about table tennis.

_____ 10. He sometimes sends her new types of paddles and tells her how to win.

Reading Activities

Building Vocabulary

You will read about how a new student, Luke, spends his free time. Before you do, let's review some vocabulary.

Activity 3. Matching Definitions

Match the words with their definitions. Work with a partner. Make guesses. Don't look at a dictionary yet. The first one is done for you.

design	three-dimensional
skeleton	software
texture	fascinated
model	process
sculpture	masterpiece

1. _____sculpture_____ objects made out of wood, clay, or metal that stand for a person or thing.

2. _____ the greatest work of an artist

3. _____ having length, width, and height

4. _____ computer programs

5. _____ a pattern or a drawing

6. _____ the feel of a surface or material

7. _____ to shape

8. _____ very interested

9. _____ a series of tasks

10. _____ bones that support a person or animal

Look at a dictionary, and check your answers. Add new words to your vocabulary notebook.

Activity 4. Reading

Read the paragraph two or three times. Read once for a basic understanding. Then read again for a full understanding.

3-D Design

by Luke Fiedorowicz

One of my hobbies is to create designs with the computer. I use three-dimensional (3-D) software. I am not trained in art, but 3-D design seems a little like creating sculpture. However, the computer can fix mistakes fast, so it is better. First, I begin with a simple shape and try to model it into something else, like a doll, a butterfly, or a skeleton. This process can take many hours. Then the hard part comes! I need to add color, texture, and light. These three things make the design look real. Light is the hardest to add. Light on the computer does not act like natural light. Movies like *Shrek* and *Ice Age* are masterpieces of 3-D design. I am fascinated by computers and what people can do with them.

Activity 5. Respond

Answer the questions about the reading. Use complete sentences. The first one is done for you.

1. What is one of Luke's hobbies? <u>One of his hobbies is to create designs</u>

    <u>with the computer.</u>

2. What does 3-D graphic design seem a little like? _____

    _____

3. Why is it better? _____

    _____

4. How does Luke begin? _____

    _____

5. How long does the process of modeling take? _____

    _____

6. What does Luke need to add to make the design look realistic? _____

    _____

7. Which of these is the hardest to add? _____

_____

8. Why is it hardest to add? _____

_____

9. Which movies are masterpieces? _____

_____

Grammar Activities

Negatives

Read these compound sentences linked with *but:*

Ana likes to bake traditional Romanian pastry, but she **does not have** much time to cook.

Yixin likes to play table tennis with her father, but she **doesn't see** him often.

Shahzad loves to travel, but he **doesn't like** to stay in big cities.

Young likes to paint with watercolors, but she **does not work** with oils much.

Frank likes his college classes, but he **doesn't like** the habits of some students.

Review these negative verb forms:

	Singular	Plural
to be	*I am not* *You are not* *He/she/it is not*	*We are not* *You are not* *They are not*
Note: *are* and *is* can be contracted: *aren't* and *isn't.*		
to have	*I do not have* *You do not have* *He/She/It does not have*	*We do not have* *You do not have* *They do not have*
Note: The helping verbs *do* and *does* can be contracted: *don't* and *doesn't.*		

All regular verbs form the present tense negative in the same way as the verb *to have.*

do / does + *not* + simple form of the verb

Activity 6. Practicing Negatives

Frank shares his likes and dislikes about studying in the United States. Change these sentences so they are negative. Put the contraction in parentheses. The first one is done for you.

1. My classes here are different from the schools in Germany. <u>My classes here are not (aren't) different from the schools in Germany.</u>

2. In German universities students take classes only in their special fields of study. _____

   _____

3. It is strange for me to take courses from other academic fields. _____

   _____

4. My friend is in an Asian literature class. _____

   _____

5. These classes interest me. _____

   _____

6. They are so different from her music major. _____

   _____

7. One thing about the university shocks me. _____

   _____

8. Some students eat and drink in class. _____

   _____

9. They put their feet on the desk in front of them sometimes. _____

   _____

10. Students in Germany show more respect. _____

    _____

Adjectives and Complements

Adjectives are words that add meaning to nouns. They can come before nouns.

Example: The *large* classes surprised the *new* student.

In this sentence, the word *large* gives more information about the noun *classes*. Also, the word *new* tells more about the noun *student*.

Adjectives can also come after the subject and after the verb *be*. Then they are called **complements.**

Examples: The classes are *large*.

The student is *new*.

Activity 7. Finding Complements

Luke shares some of his likes and dislikes about university education in the United States. Underline each adjective in the sentences that follow. Circle the verb. Circle the word not *in the verb too. The first one is done for you.*

1. I (am) happy with the U.S. university system most of the time.

2. Sometimes I am bored with the freshman courses.

3. These courses are necessary.

4. Many college students are not prepared.

5. Some high schools are sometimes not very strong.

6. The professors in the university are very friendly.

7. Their attitude is very helpful.

8. In Poland, the professors are sometimes unfriendly.

9. In Poland, only lectures, homework, and tests are important.

10. In the U.S. the connection between life and learning is good.

Writing Activities

In this chapter you will write a paragraph about your likes and dislikes. You may focus on the "likes" part of the assignment. You can describe your favorite way to spend free time, as Luke did in his paragraph about 3-D computer design. You may decide, however, to write about a difference you see, as Frank and Luke told of contrasts between U.S. universities and the universities of their countries. You may also choose to focus on the "dislikes" part of the assignment. You can describe a job you don't like to do and tell why.

First, here are some writing exercises to get you thinking.

Activity 8. Journal Topics

Are you ready to write just for fun? Write for 15 minutes without stopping on one of these topics. Try a new topic each day.

1. Write about the sports you like to play. What is your favorite? How often do you play it? Is it hard? Is there any part of the sport you dislike? Why?

2. Write about traveling. Do you like it or dislike it? What countries have you visited? What countries would you like to visit? Is there a part of travel you dislike?

3. Write about the kind of movies or television shows that you enjoy watching. Why do you like them? Give some examples of favorites. What types of shows do you dislike?

4. Write about any art that you do. Do you draw or paint? Do you like to cook? Do you like to make things? If you don't do any art, why not? What do you dislike about it?

Activity 9. Reading to Write

Read the sample paragraph by Ana. Ana likes to cook, so her paragraph is about a favorite food.

Sample Paragraph:

Pastry Baking
by Ana Oprisan

I love to bake traditional Romanian pastry, especially a kind of sweet bread. We usually serve this bread at Christmas or Easter. To make it, I use these ingredients: flour, milk, sugar, butter, eggs, and yeast. The first step is to mix the bread dough. I dissolve the yeast in warm milk with a little sugar and flour. Next I separate the eggs and mix in melted butter, sugar, milk, vanilla, and lemon zest. I use an electric mixer to blend in the flour. I then knead the bread with my hands until the dough is smooth. I cover the dough and put it in a warm place to rise. Meanwhile I make the cream filling. Chocolate is my favorite flavor. After about one hour, I take the dough and pat it into a rectangle. I spread the cream all over, almost to the edges. Then I roll the dough up, put the roll into a pan, and let it rise again. It should double in size. Finally, it is ready to bake for an hour. The house smells so good! It is time to eat the bread. That's the best part!

pastry: a type of light bread made from flour, fat, and water

ingredients: foods added to make a certain dish

yeast: a substance that makes bread rise

dissolve: to mix a solid substance into water or milk

dough: an uncooked mixture of flour, fat, water, and yeast

zest: skin of fruit used for flavoring

blend: mix evenly

knead: to work a dough with hands and fingers to make it ready for baking

rise: to make bigger

pat: to touch with a flat hand

Activity 10. Guided Sentence Practice

Write a paragraph similar to Ana's. Answer these questions in full sentences.

1. What food do you love to make?_____

_____

2. What makes this food special? _____

_____

3. What ingredients do you need? _____

_____

4. What is the first step? _____

_____

5. What do you do next?_____

_____

6. Then what do you do? _____

_____

7. Repeat questions 4-6 until you have listed all the steps. _____

_____

_____

_____

_____

8. Write any special instructions for any of the steps. Put them in order.

_____

_____

_____

_____

9. Is there a special way to eat this food?_____

_____

Activity 11. Writing a First Draft

In the space provided or on a separate page, write a paragraph about a special like (or dislike). You may use the sentences you wrote in Activity 10 on page 45 as a guide. Or you may use one of your journal topics.

_____

_____

_____

_____

_____

_____

_____

_____

_____

_____

_____

_____

_____

_____

_____

_____

_____

_____

_____

_____

_____

_____

_____

_____

Using Transition Words *First, Next, Then,* and *Finally*

In Chapter 2 we talked about linking sentences in paragraphs by repeating key words and using pronouns. In Chapter 1, you used the transition words *however* and *also* to link sentences. In paragraphs that describe steps, the transition words *first*, *next*, *then*, and *finally* can help readers follow along. Reread Ana's paragraph. Note the italicized words. These are the linking words. They help readers understand the paragraph.

Sample Paragraph:

Pastry Baking

by Ana Oprisan

I love to bake traditional Romanian pastry, especially a kind of sweet bread. We usually serve this bread at Christmas or Easter. To make it, I use flour, milk, sugar, butter, eggs, and yeast. The *first* step is to mix the bread dough. I dissolve the yeast in warm milk with a little sugar and flour. *Next* I separate the eggs and mix in melted butter, sugar, milk, vanilla, and lemon zest. I use an electric mixer to blend in the flour. I *then* knead the bread with my hands until the dough is smooth. I cover the dough and put it in a warm place to rise. *Meanwhile* I make the cream filling. Chocolate is my favorite flavor. *After* about one hour, I take the dough and pat it into a rectangle. I spread the cream all over, almost to the edges. *Then* I roll the dough up, put the roll into a pan, and let it rise again. It should double in size. *Finally,* it is ready to bake for an hour. The house smells so good! It is time to eat the bread. That's the best part!

<u>Note</u>: *The words* meanwhile *and* after *also help connect the sentences. They help make the time links clear.*

Revision

Activity 12. Peer Editing

Show your paragraph to two or three classmates. Ask them to answer the questions on the form. Your teacher will also read your paragraph.

Reader's Name _____

Writer's Name _____

1. Write in your own words what the writer likes and dislikes about his or her topic.

   _____

   _____

   _____

   _____

2. Count the number of compound structures the author uses. Write them here:

   _____

   _____

   _____

   _____

3. Where do you need or want more information? What can be added?

   _____

   _____

   _____

   _____

4. What is the best thing about this paragraph? What does the writer do well?

   _____

   _____

   _____

   _____

Activity 13. Writing Additional Drafts

Write a second draft of your paragraph on a separate sheet of paper. Use the ideas of your classmates and your teacher to write a better paragraph.

✔ Editing

It is time to check grammar. Remember to look for only one type of error at a time.

Activity 14. Working on Grammar

Look for mistakes in your paragraph. Check parts of sentences in this order:

- Check **compound structures and compound sentences.** Look at every *and, but, so,* and *or* in your writing. If you are linking independent clauses, is there a subject and verb in each clause? Check that there are commas between independent clauses. If you are linking words, are they similar parts of speech? Look for any **negative verbs.** Is the proper form used?

- Add any **transition words and linking words** to connect your sentences.

- Look at **subject-verb agreement.**

- Check for any **fragments.**

Activity 15. Preparing a Final Draft

When you feel sure that the grammar is as good as you can make it, hand in this last draft to your teacher. He or she may find more words that need to be changed. Make these changes. Then hand in a final draft.

4 Telling about Family

Photo by Ben Colman

Your family knew and loved you when you were a child. They are probably the people who know you best now. Who is your family? What are they like? Please introduce them to us!

In this chapter, you will:

- ✍ meet three new students—Endy, Martin, and Mai; and read more about Mesay.

- ✍ study complex sentences.

- ✍ learn about the past tense.

- ✍ write about your own family.

Expanding Sentences

Independent and Dependent Clauses

Remember what you learned in Chapter 2 about clauses:

clause = S + V

independent clause = complete sentence

Another type of clause is called a **dependent clause.** A dependent clause also contains a subject and a verb. However, independent clauses and dependent clauses are very different because of one word. Dependent clauses have a word in front of the subject and verb, a **subordinating conjunction.** (Remember independent clauses had a coordinating conjunction between them.) Think of subordinating conjunctions as *dependent clause words (or DCWs).*

dependent clause = DCW + S + V

Unlike independent clauses, dependent clauses cannot stand alone. They must be linked with an independent clause.

Complex Sentence = independent clause + dependent clause

Complex Sentence = S + V + DCW + s + v

There are about 20 common dependent clause words (DCWs). In this chapter you will practice with only three: *before, after,* and *when.* Look at these examples.

Simple Sentence: My uncle invited me to the U.S.

Complex Sentence: My uncle invited me to the U.S. **after my father died.**

Complex Sentence: **After my father died,** my uncle invited me to the U.S.

Note: The dependent clause can come before or after the independent clause. When the dependent clause comes before, a comma separates the two clauses.

Before and *when* work in exactly the same way, as in these examples:

When my father died, I grew up quickly.

I grew up quickly **when** my father died.

Before my father died, I was a spoiled kid.

I was a spoiled kid **before** my father died.*

*When using *before,* the first event is described in the independent clause. With *when* and *after,* the first event is in the dependent clause.

Fragments

Look at this dependent clause.

After my father died.

Alone, the dependent clause doesn't make sense. A dependent clause alone is a **fragment,** not a sentence. It needs an independent clause to complete it. If the DCW is taken away, however, the sentence becomes just a simple independent clause. The word order is the same:

<u>Example:</u>   My father died.

Activity 1. Combining Clauses with *After, Before,* and *When*

Combine each group of sentences into one complex sentence. The sentence with the DCW in parentheses is the dependent clause. The other sentence is the independent clause. Some dependent clauses will come in front of the independent clause. Some will follow. The first two are examples of each type.

1. Endy came to live with his uncle (when). He felt so lucky.

   <u>When Endy came to live with his uncle, he felt so lucky.</u>

2. He started college right away. He finished high school (after).

   <u>He started college right away after he finished high school.</u>

3. Endy decided to study in the U.S. (before). He thought about it for many months.

   _____

4. His mother cried. He left (when).

   _____

5. Mesay finished her homework (after). She watched television for a few minutes.

   _____

6. Mesay went for a walk. She ate dinner last night (before).

   _____

7. Her father got a job in the U.S. (when). The family applied for visas.

   _____

8. Her sister moved into an apartment (after). The house was quiet.

   _____

9. Martin was ten. His mother died (when).

   _____

10. Martin left Bolivia (before). He said good-bye to all his family members.

    _____

Reading Activities

Building Vocabulary

Let's look over the words you need to talk about family.

Activity 2. Matching

Match List A with List B. The first one is done for you.

List A	List B
a. mother	1. __i__ child of aunt or uncle
b. father	2. _____ mother of your father or mother
c. brother	3. _____ male child of your parents
d. sister	4. _____ female parent
e. niece	5. _____ son of your brother or sister
f. nephew	6. _____ male parent
g. uncle	7. _____ sister of your father or mother
h. aunt	8. _____ father of your father or mother
i. cousin	9. _____ daughter of your brother or sister
j. grandmother	10. _____ brother of your father or mother
k. grandfather	11. _____ female child of your parents

Activity 3. Building a Family Tree

Fill in the spaces with the proper words for family. Use the words from List A in Activity 2 on page 53. Lines show family members. Arrows show marriages. Circles are for females, and squares are for males.

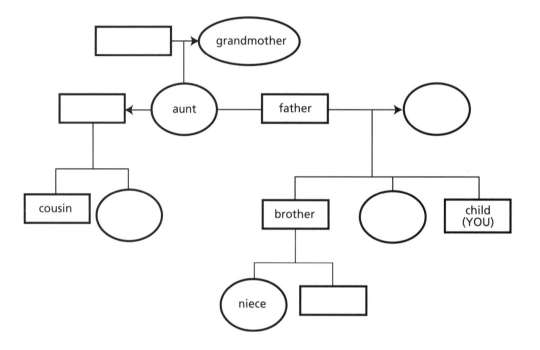

Activity 4. Readings

Three new students introduce their families to you. Also, Mesay tells more about her family. Read the paragraphs two or three times. Read once for a basic understanding. Then read again for a full understanding.

My Family in Bolivia
by Martin Urbach

I come from Santa Cruz, Bolivia. Before my parents died, we were a family of five. My mom died when I was ten. My father died suddenly two years ago when I was twenty. I have two brothers. My brothers are ten and twelve years older than me. They still live in Bolivia. They are my only family now. When I go back to Bolivia, I visit them. One of my brothers is married. He has a five-year-old daughter. Her name is Esther. She is very smart and so pretty. She tells me bedtime stories when I visit. I miss my family very much, especially Esther.

My Family

by Endy Widjaja

I am the youngest child in my family. I am twenty-two years old. In all, there are four children. I have two sisters and a brother. My father died five years ago. My mother lives in Indonesia with my brother. My sisters live near my mother too. They are both married with children. After my father died, my uncle in the U.S. asked me to come live with him. He is the oldest brother of my father. He wanted to help me, so he pays half of my tuition for the university. My family pays the other half. I work hard in school, so my family can be proud. Before I left home, I didn't like to work. Now I am more mature. I thank my uncle for this chance.

My Family

by Mesaynish Wodajo

There are six people in my family. I have a mother, a father, a sister, and two brothers. I am the oldest girl. We are from Ethiopia. My father moved to the States first. He came to study and work. He is a doctor. About a year later the rest of the family came. I was in elementary school when we moved. Now I am twenty-four years old. My sister, Etsegenet, is twenty. Samson is fifteen years old, and Kidus is eleven. We are all still in school. My sister lives in an apartment, but I still live at home with my family.

Activity 5. Respond

Answer the questions about the readings. Use complete sentences. The first one is done for you.

1. Who has the largest family with living parents and children? How many are in the family? <u>Mesay's family is the largest. She has a mother, a father, a sister, and two brothers.</u>

2. Who has the smallest family? How many are in the family?_____

3. Who is the oldest child in his or her family? _____

4. Who are the youngest in their families? _____

_____

5. Which students have lost their parents?_____

_____

_____

6. How old were they when their parents died? _____

_____

_____

7. Which students still live with family? _____

_____

8. Which student does not live with family? _____

_____

9. Which students have nieces or nephews (at least one!)? _____

_____

_____

Activity 6. Respond

Fill in what you know about Mesay's family from her paragraph.

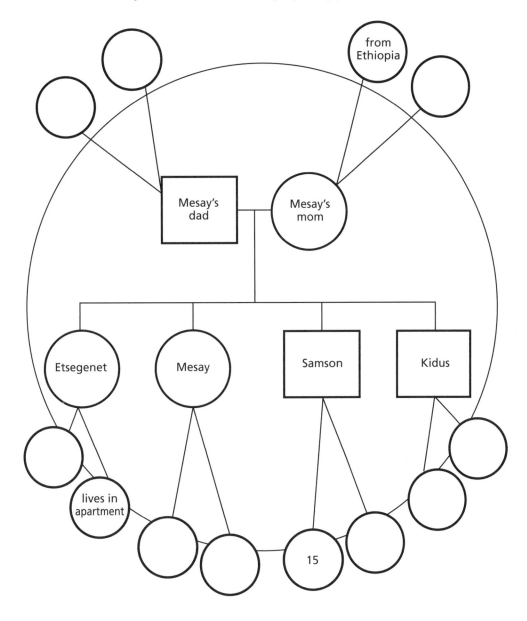

🍎 Grammar Activities

Past Tense

So far you have used the present tense to write sentences. Now you will learn how to discuss past time.

-ed Endings for Regular Verbs

Look at these regular past tense verbs.

> Example: My uncle in America **asked** me to come live with him.
>
> Example: He **wanted** to help me.
>
> Example: My father **moved** to the U.S. first.
>
> Example: My mother **died** many years ago.

Most regular past verbs are formed by adding *-ed* to the base form of the verb. If a verb already ends in *-e*, just add *-d*.

Activity 7. Putting Verbs in the Past Tense

Change the verbs in parentheses to past tense forms. The first one is done for you.

1. My family (move) _____ moved _____ to the U.S. a year after my father.

2. My father (live) _____ here alone that first year.

3. His mother (die) _____ when he was still young.

4. Then his father (pass) _____ away.

5. Endy's uncle (ask) _____ him to study at the university.

6. He (want) _____ to help the family.

Irregular Verbs

Irregular verbs do not use the *-ed* endings. These verbs need to be learned one at a time. Look at the past tense for the *be* verb. There are two forms.

Singular	Plural
was (used for *I, he, she,* and *it*)	*were* (used for *we, you,* and *they*)

> Example: When I **was** twenty, my father passed away.
>
> Example: There **were** five people in my family.

Two other common irregular verbs, *have* and *do,* only have one past tense form.

<u>**Singular and Plural**</u>

had

did

<u>Example</u>:   I **had** a hard time after my parents died.

<u>Example</u>:   They **did** their best in school.

See *Appendix G* and a dictionary for the past form of common verbs.

Activity 8. Forming Past Tense with Irregular Verbs

Change the verbs in parentheses to past tense forms. Check Appendix G or a dictionary if needed. The first one is done for you.

1. Endy _____ate_____ (eat) a big dinner on his last night in Indonesia.

2. His mother _____ (know) what he wanted to eat.

3. His brother _____ (make) a speech.

4. He _____ (say) he was happy and sad at the same time.

5. Endy _____ (feel) sad and happy too.

6. He _____ (forget) about the trip for a moment.

7. He _____ (speak) to his family about his feelings.

8. They all _____ (understand).

9. The next day Endy _____ (leave).

10. The family _____ (see) his plane take off.

Negatives in Past Tense *Was* and *Were*

Look at these negatives in past tense. *Not* follows the *be* verb. Contractions are used in spoken and informal English.

<u>Example</u>:   I **was not/wasn't** home last night.

<u>Example</u>:   You **were not/weren't** happy about that news.

Negatives in Past Tense Verbs

To make other verbs negative in the past tense, add *did* + *not* to the base form of the past tense:

did + *not* + base form of verb

Example: Martin **did not tell** Esther a bedtime story last night.

Example: Mesay and her family **did not travel** to the U.S. with her father.

Forming Questions with Past Tense Verbs

The word *did*, the helping verb in the past tense, is also used with negatives. Look at these examples:

Did she study hard?

Did you go to school today?

What did you do?

Where did you go to school?

Activity 9. Finding Errors

There is one error in each of these sentences. Find the past tense errors, and write the correct sentences on the line. Use past tense verbs. The first one is done for you.

1. My father die five years ago. <u>My father died five years ago.</u>

_____

2. Did take you the test already?_____

_____

3. What you said to the teacher? _____

_____

4. Yesterday the child want a glass of milk._____

_____

5. His brother not feel happy. _____

_____

Talking about Age in Writing

Add *-er* to an adjective when comparing two things or people.

> Example: My brother is **older** than me.

Add *-est* to an adjective when comparing three or more.

> Example: I am the **oldest** child in my family.

Use words for most short numbers in writing.

> Example: My sister is **twenty.**
>
> I am **twenty-four** years old.

Use numerals for longer numbers.

> Example: The Declaration of Independence was signed 230 years ago.

Use ordinal numbers to describe position in a family (*first, second, third,* and so on).

> Example: My sister is the **fifth** child.

Note these changes when the age is a complement and when age is an adjective before a noun.

> Example: My niece is **five years old.**
>
> I have a **five-year-old** niece.

Writing Activities

Activity 10. Journal Topics

Are you ready to write just for fun? Write for 15 minutes without stopping on one of these topics. Try a new topic each day.

1. Who was your favorite family member when you were a child? Who were you closest to? Tell an important story about that family member.

2. Who is your favorite family member now? Tell about this important family member.

3. Who is your least favorite member of your family? Why? Tell a story that explains this difficult relationship.

4. Describe a famous family from your country.

5. Describe the largest family you know. How many children were there? How was their life different from yours?

Activity 11. Guided Sentence Practice

Answer the questions in full sentences. Pay attention to all parts of the sentence, particularly subjects and verbs.

1. How many people are in your family? _____

   _____

2. What are their names and ages? _____

   _____

   _____

   _____

3. What is your age and position in the family? _____

   _____

   _____

4. Where do your family members live?_____

   _____

   _____

5. What do your family members do? _____

   _____

   _____

   _____

   _____

6. Are you close to any particular family member? Which one(s)? Why?

   _____

   _____

   _____

7. How often do you see your family members?_____

_____

_____

8. How does that make you feel? _____

_____

Activity 12. Writing a First Draft

In the space provided or on a separate page, write a paragraph about your family. Use the sentences you wrote in Activity 11 as a guide. Or you may use Mai's paragraph about her family on page 64 as a guide.

_____

_____

_____

_____

_____

_____

_____

_____

_____

_____

_____

_____

_____

_____

_____

_____

_____

_____

Sample Paragraph:

The Nguyen Family
by Mai Nguyen

I am one of nine children. My parents came to the U.S. as teenagers in 1975. They did not know each other. Soon after, they met, married, and started their own family. I am the fourth child and the only girl. I have eight brothers! The oldest is twenty-six, and the youngest is eight. When I was little, I thought the house was too noisy and dirty. I didn't like living in a house with so many boys. Now most of us work or go to school. The house is quiet most of the time. My grandparents, uncles, aunts, and cousins all live near us. We get together often on Sundays and holidays. Then the house is noisy again!

Deciding on Tense in Paragraphs and Sentences

When you write about different times, you must use different tenses. Different tenses can sometimes confuse the reader. Use other words in the sentence to make the time clear to a reader. Look at the beginning of Martin's paragraph. Present tense verbs are underlined. Past tense verbs are written in uppercase letters. And finally, time words are written in italics.

Sample Paragraph:

I <u>come</u> from Santa Cruz, Bolivia. *Before* my parents DIED, we WERE a family of five. My mom DIED *when* I WAS ten. My father DIED suddenly *two years ago when* I WAS twenty. I <u>have</u> two brothers. My brothers <u>are</u> ten and twelve years older than me. They *still* <u>live</u> in Bolivia. They <u>are</u> my only family *now*.

Notice that Martin uses present tense, then past tense, and then back to present tense. In your paragraph you will need to decide which tense fits the meaning of your sentence.

Revision

Activity 13. Peer Editing

Show your paragraph to two or three classmates. Ask them to answer the questions on the form. Your teacher will also read your paragraph.

Reader's Name _____

Writer's Name _____

1. Tell about the most interesting part of this paragraph.

   _____

   _____

   _____

2. How many times does the writer use the past tense? Write the sentences that contain past tense verbs.

   _____

   _____

   _____

   _____

3. How many complex sentences does the author use? Copy them here.

   _____

   _____

   _____

   _____

4. Where do you need or want more information? What can be added?

   _____

   _____

   _____

   _____

Activity 14. Writing Additional Drafts

Write a second draft of your paragraph on a separate sheet of paper. Use the ideas of your classmates and your teacher to write a better paragraph.

✔ Editing

It is time to check grammar. Remember to look for only one type of error at a time.

Activity 15. Working on Grammar

Look for mistakes in your paragraph. Check parts of sentences in this order:

- Check **verb tenses.** Do the past tense verbs tell about past events? Is the proper form used? Do you need **transition words and linking words** to make times clear for your readers?
- Look at any **complex sentences.** Is there a dependent clause paired with an independent clause?
- If the dependent clause comes before the independent clause, is there a **comma** between them?
- Check for any **fragments.** Be sure **subjects and verbs agree**.

Activity 16. Preparing a Final Draft

When you feel sure that the grammar is as good as you can make it, hand in this last draft to your teacher. He or she may find more words that need to be changed. Make these changes. Then hand in a final draft.

5 Telling about an Event

Storytelling is important to all people all over the world. It is also an important skill. It can help you in your personal and professional life.

In this chapter, you will:

🖎 meet two new students, Ibrahim and Yixin, and read more stories from Benito and Ana.

🖎 study complex sentences using *because, even though,* and *that.*

🖎 learn about progressive tenses.

🖎 write about an event.

Expanding Sentences

Complex Sentences with *Because* and *Even Though*

In Chapter 4 you learned about dependent clause words (DCWs, also called subordinating conjunctions) that tell about time relationships. In this chapter you will practice writing sentences with two different DCWs: *because* and *even though*. *Because* shows the cause of an action or event in the dependent clause.

RESULT   +   *because*   +   CAUSE

Example: My sister was happy because she was getting married.

because   +   CAUSE   +   RESULT

Example: *Because* our parents are from North Africa, my sister wanted a Middle Eastern wedding.

Even though tells about an event or action that is different from the information given in the independent clause.

even though + ONE EVENT + ANOTHER EVENT NOT EXPECTED
Even though she told our parents, they didn't believe her.

That is, parents can be expected to believe what their children tell them, but not in this case.

ONE EVENT   +   *even though* + A DIFFERENT EVENT
The wedding was lovely *even though* they had only two months to plan it.

That is, two months is a short time to plan a big event like a wedding. The results could have been very different.

As with any complex sentence, the dependent clause can go before or after the independent clause.

Let's look at more sentences with *because* and *even though*:

At first I didn't like college **because** I was so homesick.
Even though the city was beautiful, I didn't see its beauty.

Even though I was 18 years old, I didn't know how to shop for shoes.
I didn't know how to shop for shoes **because** my mother always bought my clothes.

Activity 1. Combining Clauses with *Because* and *Even Though*

These sentences tell about Ibrahim's sister's wedding day. Use a complex sentence to combine each group of sentences. The sentence with the DCW in parentheses is the dependent clause. The other sentence is the independent clause. Some dependent clauses will come in front of the independent clause. Some will follow. The first two are done for you.

1. Sheri didn't have a lot of time to plan it (even though). The wedding was beautiful.

   <u>Even though Sheri didn't have a lot of time to plan it, the wedding was</u>
   <u>beautiful.</u>

2. Our parents didn't believe my sister. She told them six months before (even though).

   <u>My parents didn't believe my sister even though she told them six months</u>
   <u>before.</u>

3. My sister and mother had only two months to plan the wedding (because). They had to work fast.

   _____

4. My mother loves my sister very much (because). She worked very hard.

   _____

5. They didn't have much time (even though). Everything worked out.

   _____

6. Our parents are from Egypt (because). Sheri wanted a Middle Eastern wedding.

   _____

7. Sheri's husband wanted one too. His family is Moroccan (because).

   _____

8. They served typical food from our countries. Middle Eastern cooks are hard to find (even though). _____

   _____

9. Sheri wore a traditional wedding dress. Her mother-in-law brought her one from Morocco (because). _____

   _____

10. They worked so hard (because). It was a day to remember!

    _____

Reading Activities

Building Vocabulary

Let's look over the new words you will find in Yixin's and Ibrahim's paragraphs.

Activity 2. Finding Words Alike in Meaning

Underline the word that doesn't belong in these lists. The first is done for you.
Put any new vocabulary words into your vocabulary notebook.

1. silly
     stupid
     <u>great</u>
     foolish
	4. beautiful
	     lovely
	     pretty
	     ugly
		7. wedding
		     ceremony
		     play
		     service

2. sheltered
     covered
     independent
     protected
	5. upset
	     happy
	     sad
	     ashamed
		8. caterer
		     chef
		     maid
		     cook

3. homesick
     comfortable
     unhappy
     lonely
	6. tease
	     laugh at
	     hate
	     joke with
		9. ballroom
		     place
		     hall
		     park

Activity 3. Reading

Yixin tells a story about her first year in college. Read the paragraph two or three times. Read once for a basic understanding. Then read again for a full understanding.

My New Boots

by Yixin Young

One of my most important life lessons came from a pair of boots. That sounds silly, but it is true. When I was growing up, my parents sheltered me completely. When I was eighteen, I left for college in northern China. I was living in the beautiful city of Tianjin. However, I didn't like it at all at first because I was so homesick. When the weather turned cold, I needed to buy a pair of warm boots. I went shopping but I didn't know what to buy. I bought nothing. Then I wrote a letter to my mom. I asked for her help, and she sent me a new pair of boots in the mail. Even though I was happy to wear my new boots, I was ashamed because I was still like a little child. My sister always teases me. Even now she asks, "Do you need a new pair of boots?"

Activity 4. Respond

Answer the questions about Yixin's paragraph. Use complete sentences. The first one is done for you.

1. What does Yixin think sounds silly but is true?

   One of her most important life lessons came from a pair of boots.

2. How did Yixin's parents treat her when she was growing up?

   _____

3. How did she feel about Tianjin at first?

   _____

4. What did she need when the weather turned colder?

   _____

5. What happened when she went shopping?

   _____

6. What did she buy when she went shopping?

   _____

7. How did she feel after she got her new boots?

   _____

8. What does her sister always do to her now?

   _____

9. What does her sister say to her?

   _____

Activity 5. Reading

Read Ibrahim's paragraph about his sister's wedding.

My Sister's Wedding

by Ibrahim Aboumador

My sister Sheri got married last February. Six months before the wedding, she told our parents. They didn't believe her and didn't make any plans. In December, she said that she was really serious about getting married in February. My mother went a little crazy then, because she had so much work to do in two short months! My parents are from Egypt and Sheri's husband's family is from Morocco, so they wanted a Middle Eastern wedding. Even though there wasn't a lot of time, everything worked out. My mother and Sheri found a ballroom near our house to hold the ceremony. They ordered Middle Eastern food from a caterer. They made arrangements for relatives to come from both countries. Sheri wore a traditional Moroccan wedding dress. An imam performed the ceremony. It turned out to be a beautiful day. I was happy for my mother and sister.

Activity 6. Respond

In the space write a few sentences about Sheri's wedding. Try not to look back at the reading. Write down what you remember.

_____

_____

_____

_____

_____

_____

_____

_____

_____

_____

Grammar Activities

Progressive Tenses

Progressive tenses show the progress of an action. That's why "progress" is part of the name of the tense. Progressive tenses focus on an event happening. They can be in present or past time. The form is always the same:

Be + V*ing*

Be shows the time. It can be in present or past tense, as in these examples.

Present Progressive Tense: (in progress right now)

I *am sitting* at my desk at this moment.

Past Progressive Tense: (in progress in the past)

I *was sitting* at my desk for four hours.

This tense is useful for describing past events. There is a difference between verbs in the simple past and verbs in the past progressive. Look at these examples:

Simple past (an activity that started and finished in the past)

We *had* a party to celebrate our wedding.

There *was* an earthquake that night.

Past progressive (an activity that continued over some time in the past)

All the buildings *were shaking* during the earthquake.

Often, the two tenses are used together in a sentence. The past progressive verb describes a past activity happening **during** another past event.

<u>Example</u>: When the buildings *were shaking*, we *held* each other tightly.

Activity 7. Practicing Simple Past and Past Progressive Tenses

Ana writes a paragraph about an earthquake that happened during the party after her wedding. Most of the verbs will be in the simple past tense, but a few are in the past progressive. Notice that these verbs show progress and a period of time. Fill in the blanks with the tense given in parentheses. The verb is in italics. The first one is done for you.

Earthquake!

by Ana Oprisan

One of the scariest things in my life (1) _____was_____ (**be,** simple past) an earthquake on the night of my wedding. My husband and I (2) _____ (**be,** simple past) married in a small ceremony in his small city of Barlad, Romania in September of 1986. That evening we (3) _____ (**celebrate,** simple past) with a small party of family and friends in his parents' apartment on the fourth floor. Around midnight, the floor (4) _____ (**start,** simple past) to shake. At first we (5) _____ (**not realize,** simple past) what was happening. Then someone (6) _____ (**look,** simple past) out the window. Other buildings (7) _____ (**shake,** past progressive). We (8) _____ (**have,** past progressive) an earthquake! It (9) _____ (**be,** simple past) a strong one, a 5 on the Richter Scale. There (10) _____ (**be,** simple past) some aftershocks. The lights (11) _____ (**go,** simple past) out, and all of us were very scared. I (12) _____ (**try,** simple past) to be brave and calm our guests. When the ground (13) _____ (**stop,** simple past) shaking, we lit candles and tried to recall the happiness of our wedding celebration. I remember that night now with a mixture of happiness and sadness. I (14) _____ (**be,** simple past) happy to be married, but I was very frightened.

Using Quotations or *Said That*

Compare these two sentences:

Sheri said, "**I am** getting married in February."

Sheri said that **she was** getting married in February.

Between the quotation marks are Sheri's exact words. Pronouns and tense are just as the speaker said them.

In the second sentence, the pronoun and verb tenses are changed.

S + *said* + *that* + s + v

Sheri said that **she was** getting married in February.

When you describe past events, the tense after *that* is usually in the past tense. Sometimes, *that* is left out in writing and in spoken English.

<u>Example</u>: Sheri said she was getting married in February.

Activity 8. Making Sentences with *Said That*

These sentences describe Benito's first date with his wife. Turn the quotations into dependent clauses using **said that.** *Use the past tense. Change pronouns if needed. The first two are done for you.*

1. Benito said, "I want to go to a movie with you."

   <u>Benito said that he wanted to go to a movie with her.</u>

2. Irma said, "I would* like to go."

   <u>Irma said that she would like to go.</u>

3. Then later she said, "I don't want to go." _____

   _____

4. Another day Benito said, "I want to take you to a movie." _____

   _____

5. Irma said, "I would* love to go."_____

   _____

6. On the day of the date, she said, "I am bringing a friend with me."

   _____

* *would* does not change in sentences with *said that.*

7. Benito said, "The movie would* be enjoyable for us all." _____

   _____

8. After the movie, he said, "I would* like to go get ice cream."

   _____

9. The friend said, "I need to go home now."

   _____

10. Irma said, "I would* like some ice cream too."

   _____

11. At the ice cream shop, Irma said to Benito, "I like you!"

   _____

Expanding Subjects and Objects with Prepositional Phrases

You have studied expanding simple sentences into compound sentences and some types of complex sentences. Another way to add information to sentences is to expand the nouns in sentences with prepositional phrases. The phrase is added to either the subject or the object or both. More than one prepositional phrase can be added. Look at the examples.

S + V
We were married.

S + V + preposition + noun
We were married *in a small ceremony.*

We were married *in Barlad, Romania.*

We were married *in September of 1986.*

We were married *in a small ceremony in Barlad, Romania, in September of 1986.*

S + V
The floor was shaking.

S + prep + noun + V
The floor *in the apartment* was shaking.

---

* *would* does not change in sentences with *said that.*

Activity 9. Making Sentences with Prepositional Phrases

Unscramble these sentences. Use prepositional phrases. The first one is done for you.

1. February / got / sister / in / married / my.

   <u>My sister got married in February.</u>

2. a / We / of / lot / did / work. _____

   _____

3. in / We / did / short / months / two / it. _____

   _____

4. ballroom / a / found / near / Mom / house / our. _____

   _____

5. food / ordered / We / caterer / a / from. _____

   _____

6. We / relatives / arrangements / for / made. _____

   _____

7. came / from / Egypt / They. _____

   _____

8. They / from / also / Morocco / came. _____

   _____

Writing Activities

Activity 10. Journal Topics

Are you ready to write just for fun? Write for 15 minutes without stopping on one of these topics. Try a new topic each day.

1. What past event scared you badly? Why was it so scary? Did it change you?

2. What was the happiest day of your life? Describe it in some detail. Why was it so happy?

3. What is the funniest thing that's ever happened to you? Tell about this event. Explain why it was funny.

4. Describe a time in your past where you've had to grow up and learn to be an adult. How old were you? What was going on in your life? What did you learn from this event?

Activity 11. Guided Sentence Practice

Answer the questions in full sentences. Pay attention to all parts of the sentence, particularly subjects and verbs.

1. What is one of the most important events of your life? _____

   _____

2. How old were you when this happened? _____

   _____

3. What were you doing at this time? _____

   _____

4. How did it start? _____

   _____

5. Then what happened? _____

   _____

   _____

6. What happened in the end? _____

   _____

   _____

7. How did you feel? _____

_____

_____

8. How did the event change you? _____

_____

_____

Activity 12. Writing a First Draft

In the space provided or on a separate page, write a paragraph about an important event. You may use the sentences you wrote in Activity 11 as a guide. Or you may use Benito's paragraph about his first date with his wife on page 80.

_____

_____

_____

_____

_____

_____

_____

_____

_____

_____

_____

_____

_____

_____

_____

_____

Sample Paragraph:

First Date

by Benito Sanchez

The most important event in my life was my first date with my future wife, Irma. We were working together in a factory in Venezuela when I asked her to go with me to see a movie. She said yes and then called later to say no. I asked her again another day. Even though she came that time, I was disappointed because she brought a friend. I wanted to be alone with Irma. However, the three of us enjoyed the movie. After the movie, I invited them both to go for ice cream. The friend said no and went home. Finally I was alone with Irma! She said then that she was scared because she liked me so much. After six months we were a couple. Two years later we married.

Topic Sentences in Paragraphs

Paragraphs often start with a sentence that explains what the paragraph is about in a general way. Look at the opening sentences of the student paragraphs you have read in this chapter:

> One of the scariest things in my life was an earthquake on the night of my wedding.

> One of my most important life lessons came from a pair of boots.

> The most important event in my life was my first date with my future wife, Irma.

These types of sentences are called topic sentences. The rest of the sentences in the paragraph explain the topic sentence in more detail.

Activity 13. Writing Topic Sentences

Review the paragraphs you have written so far in this course. Check to see that you have written good topic sentences. A good topic sentence should prepare the reader for what is coming up in the paragraph. If you can make a topic sentence clearer, rewrite it. Use the sentences in Activity 11 as a guide.

Revision

Activity 14. Peer Editing

Show your paragraph to two or three classmates. Ask them to answer the questions on the form. Your teacher will also read your paragraph.

Reader's Name _____

Writer's Name _____

1. In a few words describe the event in this paragraph.

    _____

    _____

    _____

2. Is there a topic sentence? If yes, write it here. If not, write one here.

    _____

    _____

3. Is there any part of the paragraph that is unclear? Write any questions that you have for the author.

    _____

    _____

    _____

4. Does the author use any sentences with *because* or *even though*? Copy them here.

    _____

    _____

    _____

5. Where do you need or want more information? What can be added?

    _____

    _____

    _____

Activity 15. Writing Additional Drafts

Write a second draft of your paragraph on a separate sheet of paper. Use the ideas of your classmates and your teacher to write a better paragraph.

✔ Editing

It is time to check grammar. Remember to look for only one type of error at a time.

Activity 16. Working on Grammar

Look for mistakes in your paragraph. Check parts of sentences in this order:

- Check **verb tenses.** Are the verbs telling about past events in the past tense? Is the proper form used? Are **progressive verbs** used to show events in progress?
- Look at any **complex sentences.** Is there a dependent clause paired with an independent clause? Is the punctuation correct?
- Does your paragraph begin with a **topic sentence?**
- Check for any **fragments.** Be sure **subjects and verbs agree.**

Activity 17. Preparing a Final Draft

When you feel sure that the grammar is as good as you can make it, hand in this last draft to your teacher. He or she may find more words that need to be changed. Make these changes. Then hand in a final draft.

6 Telling about Heroes

© Copyright Kreutz Photography

Heroes inspire us to live better lives. They are important people, not only to us but to others. We should share their stories, so that others can be inspired.

In this chapter, you will:

↳ read more stories from Mesay, Benito, and Eleomarques.

↳ study complex sentences using *think that, believe that,* and *know that.*

↳ learn about Verb + V*ing* and Verb + *to* + Verb forms.

↳ write about a hero.

📐 Expanding Sentences

Complex Sentences with *Think, Believe,* and *Know*

Three very common verbs often form complex sentences. Look at these examples:

> I think (that) my cousin Seluf was a brave woman.
>
> I believe (that) Miguel Cabrera is a great baseball player.

Look at the structure of these sentences:

> S + V + *(that)*   +   s   +   v
> I know (that) my English teacher is very dedicated.

The word *that* is the DCW, or the word that begins a dependent clause. It is often left out in writing and in spoken English.

Activity 1. Combining Clauses with *Think, Believe,* and *Know*

The sentences tell about one of Benito's heroes, Miguel Cabrera. Cabrera is a major league baseball player. Combine each of the two sentences into a complex one using the DCW **that. That** *may be left out. The first one is done for you.*

1. I think (that). Miguel Cabrera is one of the best baseball players today.

   <u>I think Miguel Cabrera is one of the best baseball players today.</u>

2. I know (that). He is still very young.

   _____

3. I believe (that). He was still a teenager when he turned professional.

   _____

4. I think (that). He started his career as a shortstop.

   _____

5. I believe (that). He plays left field now.

   _____

6. I think (that). He has a very good arm.

   _____

7. I know (that). He can throw the ball hard.

   _____

8. I believe (that). He is a good batter too.

   _____

9. I believe (that). He is the youngest player to have the most home runs in major league baseball.

   _____

   _____

10. I think (that). Miguel Cabrera is at the start of a very successful career.

    _____

Reading Activities

Building Vocabulary

Let's look over the new words you will find in Eleomarques's paragraph on page 86.

Activity 2. Matching Definitions

Match words in List A with the definitions in List B. The first one is done for you. Put any new words into your vocabulary notebook.

List A	List B
a. conversational	1. _____ surprised
b. grateful	2. _____ thankful
c. dedicated	3. _____ to change into another language
d. scholarship	4. _____ a gift of money for study
e. shocked	5. _a_ spoken
f. patient	6. _____ to learn quickly
g. translate	7. _____ pleasant, fun
h. make progress	8. _____ hard-working
i. enjoyable	9. _____ to help someone to do something
j. encourage	10. _____ gentle, kind

Activity 3. Reading

Leo tells about a favorite teacher. Read the paragraph two or three times. Read once for a basic understanding. Then read again for a full understanding.

Norma, My Teacher

by Eleomarques Ferreira Rocha

My hero is an English teacher I had in high school in Brazil. I had taken English for many years but still could not speak it very well. This teacher, Norma Silva, offered to teach conversational English every day during lunch. Lunch is very important to most Brazilians. I thought she was very dedicated to give it up. Ms. Silva wanted to help us. Most of the students in the class were poor. She knew English would help us get scholarships and find jobs. The first day of class I was shocked because I could not understand very many words in English. None of us could speak much English. Ms. Silva was very patient and translated into Portuguese only a little. When she knew we knew the words, she only used English. We made good progress. She also made the classes enjoyable with songs and fun stories. She encouraged us to bring in the English that we found in our daily lives. I learned so much that year. Now I use English every day. I feel very grateful to Norma Silva, my hero.

Activity 4. Respond

Answer the questions about Eleomarques's paragraph. Use complete sentences. The first one is done for you.

1. Who is Leo's hero?

   Leo's hero is an English teacher in Brazil, Norma Silva.

2. What did Norma Silva do for Leo?

   _____

3. Why did Leo think she was dedicated?

   _____

4. Why did Ms. Silva want to help poor students?

   _____

5. How did he feel on the first day of class?

   _____

6. How well did Leo speak English at the beginning of her class?

   _____

7. When did Ms. Silva use only English?

   _____

8. How did Ms. Silva make the classes interesting?

   _____

9. What were the students asked to bring in?

   _____

10. How does Leo feel about his teacher, Norma Silva?

    _____

 # Grammar Activities

Verb + *Ving* Forms and Verb + *To* + Verb

Another way to add information to sentences is to add to the verb. Verbs can be followed by two forms, called gerunds and infinitives. Look at the patterns of these forms:

V = base form of verb

Gerund = V + *ing*	Example: *going*
Infinitive = *to* + V	Example: *to go*

Gerunds and **infinitives** act like nouns in sentences. They can be subjects, objects, or objects of prepositions. In this book we will study them as objects. As objects, these forms follow verbs. Some verbs take both the *Ving* and the *to* + V forms. Some verbs take only one form, either the *Ving* or the *to* + V form. Some common verbs and their patterns are:

Verb + *Ving* (Verbs followed by gerunds)		
enjoy	keep	quit
finish	miss	
Verb + *to* + Verb (Verbs followed by infinitives)		
decide	learn	seem
expect	need	want
hope	plan	
Verb + *Ving* and Verb + *to* + Verb (Verbs followed by either)		
begin	like	hate
start	love	try

Activity 5. Verbs Plus Gerunds or Infinitives

*Follow the verb in each sentence with the proper form, either **Ving** or a **to + V.**
Use the verb in the parentheses. The first one is done for you.*

1. Cabrera wanted (play) _____to play_____ in the major leagues at a young age.

2. I enjoy (watch) _____ Miguel Cabrera play baseball.

3. He plans (work) _____ hard for many years.

4. Norma Silva loved (eat) _____ a big lunch like most Brazilians.

5. But she decided (work) _____ with students during lunch.

6. She hoped (teach) _____ them conversational English.

7. With English they could expect (get) _____ money for study.

8. When the students began (study) _____, they could barely speak a word of English.

9. However, they really liked (be) _____ in her classes.

10. The students kept (work) _____ on their English.

Renaming Phrases

In Chapter 5 you learned about expanding nouns with prepositional phrases. There are other ways to expand nouns. Renaming phrases follow nouns. The phrase tells more about the first noun and "renames" it. Look at these examples:

Miguel Cabrera, *an excellent athlete*, is my favorite baseball player.

He started his career as a shortstop, *a difficult position*.

My teacher, *Norma Silva*, is my hero.

She worked through lunch, *an important meal in Brazil*.

Renaming phrases are set off by commas.

Activity 6. Making Sentences with Renaming Phrases

Read about Mesay's cousin. Complete the sentences making the sentence in parentheses a renaming phrase. The first one is done for you.

1. (My cousin is Seble Heluf.)

   My cousin, _____Seble Heluf_____, is my hero.

2. (Cancer is a terrible sickness.)

   She died at the age of 28 from cancer, _____.

3. (Nine years is a long time.)

   She was sick off and on for nine years, _____.

4. (Seble was a kind person.)

   Seble, _____, treated me like a younger sister.

5. (Long hours were a difficult job for her.)

   Even when she was sick, she worked long hours, _____

   _____.

6. (Seble was a hard worker.)

   Seble, _____, never complained.

7. Money was a gift from her to her friends.

   She gave away most of her money, _____.

8. A lot of money is ten thousand dollars.

   After her death, her friends raised a lot of money, _____,

   to send her body back to Ethiopia for her funeral.

Writing Activities

Activity 7. Journal Topics

Are you ready to write just for fun? Write for 15 minutes without stopping on one of these topics. Try a new topic each day.

1. Who is the person in your family you respect the most? Why? Is there a good story about this person?

2. Who is the person among your friends you respect the most? Why? Tell about this person's qualities that you most admire.

3. Who is the person in all your years of schooling you respect the most? Why? Give some detail.

4. Who is the famous person you respect the most? In what way would you like to be like this person?

5. Who is the athlete you respect the most? Why? What has he or she done that you admire?

Activity 8. Guided Sentence Practice

Answer the questions in full sentences. Pay attention to all parts of the sentence, particularly subjects and verbs.

1. Who is your hero? _____

   _____

2. What is the main reason this person is your hero? _____

   _____

3. When did you meet or first know of this person?_____

   _____

4. What did you think of him or her at the first meeting? _____

   _____

5. Has your opinion changed in the time that you have known him or her?

   _____

   _____

6. What are some examples of his or her character? _____

   _____

   _____

7. Is there a short story about your hero that shows this character? Write it here._____

_____

_____

_____

8. What sentence sums up this person's importance to you? _____

_____

_____

Activity 9. Writing a First Draft

In the space provided or on a separate page, write a paragraph about a hero. Use the sentences you wrote in Activity 8 as a guide. Or you may use Mesay's and Benito's paragraphs about their heroes that follow.

_____

_____

_____

_____

_____

_____

_____

_____

_____

_____

Sample Paragraphs:

Seble Heluf, A Hero for Love

by Mesaynish Wodajo

My cousin, Seble Heluf, is my hero. She died early from cancer at the age of twenty-eight, but she lived a full life. Even though she was sick off and on for nine years, she still went to school and worked. She was seven years older than me. She took care of me when I was a baby. She would fix my hair like an older sister. When I grew older, Seble showed me how to be a kind person. She worked hard and enjoyed life. She never complained. When she felt well, she worked sixteen-hour days and gave most of her money away. She would cook for others and do other little kindnesses. After her death, her friends raised ten thousand dollars to take her body back to Ethiopia. I know now that success does not always mean having a lot of money. Seble was successful in love. She was an inspiration for me and for many other people.

My Baseball Hero
by Benito Sanchez

I love baseball. My hero is Miguel Cabrera. He plays for the Florida Marlins. He turned professional while he was still a teenager, but he was already an excellent athlete. He still is. He started his career as a shortstop. Now he plays in the left field. He has a very good arm and can throw the ball hard. He is a good batter too. He is the youngest player to have the most home runs in major league baseball. I think he is at the start of a very successful career. I love to watch Miguel Cabrera play baseball.

Writing Concluding Sentences

Paragraphs often end with a sentence that repeats in some way what the paragraph has been about. This concluding sentence works together with the topic sentence of the paragraph. Look at the concluding sentences of the student paragraphs you have read in this chapter:

> *She (Seble) was an inspiration for me and for many other people.*
>
> *I owe a great deal to Norma Silva, my hero.*
>
> *I love to watch Miguel Cabrera play baseball.*

Activity 10. Writing Concluding Sentences

Review the paragraphs you have written so far in this course. Check to see that you have written good concluding sentences. A good concluding sentence should remind the reader about the main idea of the paragraph. If you can make the concluding sentence clearer, rewrite it. Use the sentences in the previous section as a guide.

Revision

Activity 11. Peer Editing

Show your paragraph to two or three classmates. Ask them to answer the questions on the form. Your teacher will also read your paragraph.

Reader's Name _____

Writer's Name _____

1. Do you think this person is a hero? Why or why not?

   _____

   _____

   _____

2. What particular story shows the person is a hero? Write it in your own words here.

   _____

   _____

   _____

   _____

3. Does the author use any sentences with *think, believe,* or *know (that)*? Copy them here.

   _____

   _____

   _____

   _____

4. Where do you need or want more information? What can be added?

   _____

   _____

   _____

   _____

Activity 12. Writing Additional Drafts

Write a second draft of your paragraph on a separate sheet of paper. Use the ideas of your classmates and your teacher to write a better paragraph.

✔ Editing

It is time to check grammar. Remember to look for only one type of error at a time.

Activity 13. Working on Grammar

Look for mistakes in your paragraph. Check parts of sentences in this order:

- Look at **complex sentence structure.** Is the DCW used correctly? Are dependent clauses linked with independent clauses? Check punctuation.
- Check **verbs.** Are there any verbs followed by other verbs? Is the correct form used—either V + *to* + V or V + V*ing?*
- Check **verb tenses.** Are the proper tense and form used?
- Does your paragraph end with a **concluding sentence?**
- Check for any **fragments.** Be sure **subjects and verbs agree.**

Activity 14. Preparing a Final Draft

When you feel sure that the grammar is as good as you can make it, hand in this last draft to your teacher. He or she may find more words that need to be changed. Make these changes. Then hand in a final draft.

7 Telling about the Future and Getting Older

What kind of older person would you like to be? As we age, we don't stop living. Older people can inspire us to live our lives to the fullest. Let's share some stories about some super seniors.

In this chapter, you will:

- ➷ read stories from Young, Mai, Martin, and Shahzad.

- ➷ study complex sentences using *that, which,* and *who.*

- ➷ learn more about Verb + Verb forms.

- ➷ write about an older person you respect.

Expanding Sentences

Complex Sentences with *That, Who,* and *Which*

That, who, and *which* are dependent clause words (DCWs). The dependent clauses they create are like adjectives. In fact, these kinds of dependent clauses are called **adjective clauses.** Like an adjective, an adjective clause gives more information about a noun. The clause follows the noun. In this book, use *who* for people, *which* for animals and things, and *that* for either. (Some people just use *that* and *who* for simplicity's sake.) Look at these examples:

S (sing) + s + v   +   V
The girl **who is sitting over there** is my sister.

S (pl) + s + v   +   V
Dogs **that bark a lot** can be a problem.

S (sing)   +   s + v   +   V
The post office, **which is next to the library downtown,** opens at 8:00.*

In all of these examples the DCW, the *who, that,* or *which,* is the subject of the dependent clause. The verb that follows agrees with the noun before the clause.

In some adjective clauses, there is another subject besides the DCW. In these sentences the DCW can be left out, as in these examples:

S   +   DCW + s   +   v + V
The older person **that I most respect** is my grandfather.

The older person **I most respect** is my grandfather.

The kind of dog **which my friend likes best** is a German Shepherd.

The kind of dog **my friend likes best** is a German Shepherd.

Activity 1. Identifying Adjective Clauses

The sentences tell about the older person Young most admires. Aunt Virginia is the aunt of Young's husband. Each sentence has one adjective clause. Underline the clause and circle the noun it follows. The first one is done for you.

1. My husband's Aunt Virginia is the older (person) that I most respect.

2. She was a woman who knew how to live.

3. She married a man who was a colonel in the Air Force.

4. After World War II, they moved to a German city that was very poor.

* Use commas to separate adjective clauses that give extra information.

5. She organized a club that helped poor German girls.

6. She also moved to Japan with her husband who was stationed there.

7. Aunt Virginia started a school for Japanese women who wanted to learn English.

8. Aunt Virginia told exciting stories that made my husband want to travel to the Orient.

9. She loved to read books that were full of adventure.

10. She loved visiting places that were far away.

Activity 2. Combining Sentences with *That, Who,* and *Which*

*The pairs of sentences tell more about Aunt Virginia. Combine each into a complex sentence using an adjective clause. The second sentence of each pair will become the dependent clause. Choose the correct DCW, either **who, that, or which.** The first one is done for you.*

1. Aunt Virginia was a woman kind to me and my husband. This woman was kind to everyone.

   Aunt Virginia was a woman who was kind to everyone.

2. She gave wonderful parties. The parties were quite large.

   _____

3. She hired musicians. These musicians were the best in the city.

   _____

4. She served food. The food was delicious.

   _____

5. Sometimes she invited us to small dinners. These small dinners were for family only.

   _____

6. At the age of 83, her husband had a stroke. This stroke left him very weak.

   _____

7. For nine years Aunt Virginia cared for him in their house. Their house became like a hospital.

   _____

8. She nursed her husband with a love. This love was patient and kind.

   _____

9. She died soon after her husband with a peace. That peace was beautiful.

   _____

10. I will always admire this woman. This woman changed my life.

    _____

Reading Activities

Building Vocabulary

Let's look over the new words you will find in Martin's and Shahzad's paragraphs that follow.

Activity 3. Using Adjective Clauses to Define

The sentences use adjective clauses to explain the new vocabulary of this chapter. The adjective clauses are in bold. Fill in the blanks with one of these words. The first one is done for you.

attitude	advice
challenge	adore
opportunity	coworker
overcome	strict
inspire	encourage

1. A _____coworker_____ is a person **who works with another worker.**

2. An _____ is a situation **that can make it possible for someone to do something.**

3. An _____ is a state of mind **that shows a certain view of life.**

4. A _____ is something **that is new or difficult to do.**

5. To _____ is an action **that helps others try new and difficult things.**

6. To _____ someone is a feeling **that is strong love.**

7. To _____ is an action **that makes others want to do something good.**

8. _____ is an opinion **that can help others make a decision.**

9. To feel _____ is to feel **that a situation cannot continue.**

10. A person **who is** _____ wants others to follow rules.

Activity 4. Finding Subjects and Verbs in Adjective Clauses

*Now look back at the adjective clauses in bold in Activity 3. Try to label the subject and verb in each dependent clause. Remember that in adjective clauses the DCW (**who, which,** or **that**) is often the subject of the dependent clause! Follow this example:*

           S   V

A colonel in the Air Force is a person **who has a lot of power.**

Now can you find the main subject and main verb? Follow this example:

S   V

A colonel in the Air Force is a person **who has a lot of power.**

Activity 5. Reading

Martin writes about an older person he admires. Read the paragraph two or three times. Read first for a basic understanding. Then read again for a full understanding.

Seventy Years Young

by Martin Urbach

When I get old, I hope to be like my seventy-year-old friend Mary. Her husband died a few years ago, and she decided to go back to school to get a degree in music. She has children and grandchildren to keep her busy, but she wanted a challenge in her life. Mary has a great attitude. She is at school every day at 8 o'clock doing homework. She has bad knees but never minds walking up the stairs. She looks at problems as opportunities. Sometimes I feel overcome with worry about my studies, but Mary keeps me going. She gives me good advice. I try to help her too. Sometimes I help her with her computer. Mary is old enough to be my grandmother, but we are still the best of friends.

Activity 6. Respond

Answer the questions about Martin's paragraph. Use complete sentences. The first one is done for you.

1. Who does Martin want to be like when he gets old?

    He wants to be like his seventy-year-old friend Mary.

2. What did Mary decide to do after her husband died?

    _____

3. What keeps Mary busy?

    _____

4. What did Mary want?

    _____

5. Martin gives three examples of Mary's great attitude. Write them here.

    _____

    _____

    _____

6. How does Mary keep Martin going?

    _____

7. How does Martin help Mary?

    _____

Activity 7. Reading

Shahzad writes about his grandfather. Read the paragraph two or three times. Read first for a basic understanding. Then read again for a full understanding.

My Grandfather
by Shahzad Arain

My grandfather inspires me. In Pakistan he worked for the government. He was a tax official who was very honest and helpful. He loved people, and people loved him. Coworkers, friends, and neighbors all respected him. I adored him. When I was a young child, he taught me right from wrong. He taught me the proper way to speak and how to behave. He was kind but strict with me. When I grew older, he encouraged me to work in school for the highest grades. He taught me to go to sleep early at night and get up early in the morning. In high school I started waking up at 4 or 5 A.M. to study, and I started making excellent grades. He died before I graduated, but I know he was proud of me. Now in college I still plan my time in this way. I am who I am because of my grandfather.

Activity 8. Respond

Answer the questions about Shahzad's paragraph. Use complete sentences. The first one is done for you.

1. What kind of tax official was Shahzad's grandfather?

   He was a tax official who was very honest and helpful.

2. Who respected him besides Shahzad?

   _____

3. When Shahzad was young, what did his grandfather teach him?

   _____

4. What advice did he give to Shahzad when he was grew older?

   _____

5. What did he teach Shahzad?

   _____

6. What happened when Shahzad started waking up at 4 or 5 A.M. to study?

   _____

7. What does Shahzad still do in college?

   _____

Grammar Activities

Let's learn about some of the verbs you may use to write your own paragraphs about special older people.

Using the Verbs *Can* and *Could*

Can is a verb that is used with other verbs to show that a certain action is possible. *Can* shows ability or possibility. The verb that follows *can* tells what the action is. The second verb does not have any endings and never changes from the base form. Look at these examples:

> *can* + V (no endings)
> I **can study** the way that my grandfather taught me.
> Martin **can help** Mary with her computer.

Could is the past tense of *can* when it means ability or possibility. It is also followed by a base form verb:

> *could* + V (no endings)
> Because she was a strong person, Aunt Virginia **could help** others

Using the Verbs *Hope* and *Would Like*

The verbs *hope* and *would like* are verbs that must be followed by infinitives. *Hope* tells about a dream or a wish for the future. *Would like* tells about a present wish or a future wish. Both verbs are followed by *to* + another verb (the infinitive). Look at these examples:

> *hope* + *to* + V
> One day Shahzad **hopes to be** respected by his coworkers.

> *would like* + *to* + V
> Martin **would like to thank** Mary for her kindness.

Activity 9. Using *Can, Hope,* and *Would Like*

Fill in the blank with the verb in parentheses. Use either the base form of the verb or the infinitive. The first one is done for you.

1. Aunt Virginia hoped (make) ___to make___ a difference in the world.

2. Young hopes (be) _____ like her when she gets older.

3. She hopes (help) _____ others and be active in her old age.

4. Shahzad would like (thank) _____ his grandfather for his good advice.

5. His grandfather could (love) _____ all people.

6. Shahzad hopes (earn) _____ excellent grades in college.

7. He can (go) _____ to bed early and wake up early to study.

8. Mary could (complain) _____ about her knees, but she doesn't.

9. Mary hopes (study) _____ music for the rest of her life.

10. Martin would like (be) _____ like Mary when he is in his seventies.

Writing Activities

Activity 10. Journal Topics

Are you ready to write just for fun? Write for 15 minutes without stopping on one of these topics. Try a new topic each day.

1. Who is the oldest person you know? What kind of life does he/she lead? Tell a story about this person.

2. What kind of older person do you <u>not</u> want to be? Why not?

3. What is the best thing about growing older? What are the things you are most looking forward to? Why?

4. What is the worst thing about growing older? Why? Is there anything that scares you about old age?

Activity 11. Guided Sentence Practice

Answer the questions in full sentences. Pay attention to all parts of the sentence, particularly subjects and verbs.

1. What older person do you most admire and respect? _____

    _____

2. What is the most important reason you admire this person? _____

    _____

3. Give an example of this quality. _____

    _____

4. Are there other reasons? List them. _____

    _____

    _____

5. Give examples of these qualities. _____

    _____

    _____

6. Give other details of this person's life that you admire. _____

    _____

    _____

7. In what way has this person inspired you to change your life now?

    _____

    _____

8. In what way would you like to be like this person when you are older?

    _____

    _____

Activity 12. Writing a First Draft

In the space provided or on a separate page, write a paragraph about an older person you respect. Use the sentences you wrote in Activity 11 as a guide. Or you may use Young's paragraph about Aunt Virginia that follows.

_____

_____

_____

_____

_____

_____

_____

_____

_____

_____

_____

Sample Paragraph:

Aunt Virginia

by Young Kim

The older person that I most respect is my husband's Aunt Virginia. She was born in America and married a colonel in the Air Force. When her husband was sent to Germany after World War II, Aunt Virginia followed him and organized a club to help poor girls. When he was sent to Japan, Aunt Virginia followed him again. In Japan she earned a degree at the university and taught English to wives of Japanese officers. When I met her, she was much older but she was still active. She loved books and loved to travel. She traveled to China in the very early years when it was first open to foreigners. Aunt Virginia was very kind to me and my husband. She invited us to her house for parties. Her parties were quite large. She hired musicians and served wonderful food. After her husband had a stroke at the age of 83, she cared for him at home for nine long years. I never heard her complain. She died shortly after her husband. I would like to be like her when I am old. I want to be active and help others.

Adding Supporting Details

You have studied about topic sentences and concluding sentences. The sentences that go between these two types of sentences are also important. These sentences give information, the details, that supports the topic sentence. The more detail a paragraph has, the better it is. In the paragraph that follows, Mai tells how she respects her mother. She wants to be like her because she cares so much about family. To show how she cares about family, Mai gives these details:

- her escape from Vietnam with her family
- her marriage to a Vietnamese man
- how she wants her children to be proud of their Vietnamese heritage
- how she wants them to live close
- how she wants to take care of her grandchildren
- how she wants to cook Vietnamese food for her grandchildren and teach them the Vietnamese language

All of these details support Mai's main idea in the paragraph. These details show how Mai's mother cares so much about family. Now read the paragraph in full that follows.

Sample Paragraph:

My Mother
by Mai Nguyen

When I get older, I would like to be like my mother. For my mother, family is the most important thing. She escaped from Vietnam with her family in 1975. Then she married my father, who is also Vietnamese. She brought us up to be proud of our Vietnamese heritage. Sometimes we argue with her. We tell her that we are Americans now. She always replies, "Your face, your hair, and your whole body are Vietnamese." My mother would like us all to live in the same city and even in the same neighborhood when we get married and leave home. She doesn't want us to scatter like American families. When she gets to be an old woman, she says that she wants to take care of our children, her future grandchildren. She will cook Vietnamese food for them and speak Vietnamese to them. I am very happy that my mother has taught me about my culture and wants to teach the next generation. I respect her for keeping our family so close.

Activity 13. Adding Supporting Details

Complete the paragraph with your own sentences. Make sure your sentences give lots of supporting detail.

When I am older, I would like to travel all around the world._____

_____

_____

_____

_____

_____

_____

_____

_____

_____

_____

_____

_____

_____

After all this traveling, I can relax and enjoy my old age.

Revision

Activity 14. Peer Editing

Show your paragraph to two or three classmates. Ask them to answer the questions on the form. Your teacher will also read your paragraph.

Reader's Name _____

Writer's Name _____

1. Why does the writer respect this older person?

   _____

   _____

   _____

   _____

2. Does the writer tell a story about this older person? Write it in your own words here.

   _____

   _____

   _____

   _____

3. Does the author use any sentences with adjective clauses? Copy them here.

   _____

   _____

   _____

   _____

4. Where do you need or want more information? What can be added?

   _____

   _____

   _____

   _____

Activity 15. Writing Additional Drafts

Write a second draft of your paragraph on a separate sheet of paper. Use the ideas of your classmates and your teacher to write a better paragraph.

✔ Editing

It is time to check grammar. Remember to look for only one type of error at a time.

Activity 16. Working on Grammar

Look for mistakes in your paragraph. Check parts of sentences in this order:

- Look at **adjective clauses.** Is the DCW a subject? Is the DCW correct (*who* for people, *which* for things, and *that* for either)? Does the verb agree with the noun in front of the clause? Are commas around any adjective clause that gives extra information?
- Check **verbs.** Do you use *can, will, hope to,* or *would like to*? Is the verb that follows in the base form, without endings?
- Check other **verbs.** Are the proper tense and form used?
- Does your paragraph begin with a topic sentence and end with a **concluding sentence?**
- Check for any **fragments.** Be sure **subjects and verbs agree.**

Activity 17. Preparing a Final Draft

When you feel sure that the grammar is as good as you can make it, hand in this last draft to your teacher. He or she may find more words that need to be changed. Make these changes. Then hand in a final draft.

8 Telling about Future Work

What is your ideal job? What kind of work would you like to do for the rest of your life? Let's read and write paragraphs about some interesting jobs.

In this chapter, you will:

✎ read stories from Shahzad, Ibrahim, Frank, and Endy.

✎ study compound-complex sentences.

✎ learn about future verb forms.

✎ write about your own ideal job.

Expanding Sentences

Compound-Complex Sentences

We have studied three kinds of sentences so far: **simple, compound,** and **complex sentences.** There is a fourth type of sentence, the **compound-complex sentence.** A compound-complex sentence contains both a compound sentence and a complex sentence. Look at these examples:

S   +   V   +   DCW   +   s   +   v   , and S + V

I always worked hard in school **because** my father wanted it, **and** I liked to please him. (compound-complex)

The pattern of this compound-complex sentence is:

independent clause + dependent clause + independent clause.

Compound-complex sentences can also follow this pattern:

dependent clause + independent clause + independent clause

Example:

DCW +   s   +   v   , S + V, and   S + V

When my father asked me to work hard, I did, **and** my grades got better.

Activity 1. Combining Compound and Complex Sentences.

The sentences tell about a dream that Shahzad has to become a doctor. Combine these sentences into sentences that contain one compound sentence and one complex sentence. Use the words in parentheses for combining. The first one is done for you.

1. Shahzad always wanted to be a doctor. (because) His grandfather wanted him to become one. (and) He encouraged him to study hard.

   Shahzad always wanted to be a doctor because his grandfather wanted

   him to become one, and he encouraged him to study hard.

2. His grandfather passed away. (when) Shahzad was in high school. (but) His dream is still alive. _____

   _____

3. (Even though) Shahzad was always good in math and biology. He did not have a high enough score to get into medical school in Pakistan. (so) His father encouraged him to study computer science.

    _____

    _____

4. (When) His father left for the U.S. He asked Shahzad to come with him. (and) Shahzad said he would think about it.

    _____

    _____

5. (Even though) Shahzad did not want to leave Pakistan at that time. He knew it would be a good opportunity. (and) He would get a good job.

    _____

    _____

6. Now Shahzad is working on a degree in computer science. (but) He cannot stop thinking. (that) He could still be a doctor. _____

    _____

7. (Because) He still wants to help people get well. He thinks. (that) Computer work will soon bore him. _____

    _____

8. (After) He works a few years. He will take a few science courses. (and) He can apply to medical school in the U.S. _____

    _____

Reading Activities

Building Vocabulary

Activity 2. Words for Work

With a partner, look at the list of words used to talk about work. Discuss any differences in meaning and style. Put any new words into your vocabulary notebook.

job	work	career
profession	occupation	employment

Now let's look at the new words you will find in the paragraphs.

Activity 3. Defining Work Vocabulary

Work with a partner to fill in the words into the paragraph. Make guesses. Do not look at a dictionary yet. The first one is done for you.

goal	prefer	management
ideal	decision	comfortable
reputation	corporate chain	intern

My ① _____goal_____ is to get a degree in business. This was a big ② _____ for me, and I thought for a long time about what kind of work that I would like. I decided that the business world would be ③ _____ for me. I am interested in ④ _____ because I like managing things and people. I ⑤ _____ to be in charge. I also like to help people. Helping people to be ⑥ _____ in their work is an important job. After I get my degree, I would like to work as an ⑦ _____. Interns are workers in training. I hope to work for a large ⑧ _____ _____. A large company with many locations will give me lots of opportunities. I hope to have a good ⑨ _____ as a hard worker in this first job.

Look up any words you don't understand. Write new words in your vocabulary notebook.

Activity 4. Reading

Endy writes about his dream job as a hotel manager near his home in Indonesia. Read the paragraph two or three times. Read first for a basic understanding. Then read again for a full understanding.

My Ideal Job

by Endy Widjaja

I am interested in business. Now I am working on a degree in hotel, restaurant, and tourism management. Someday I want to be a hotel manager. I like hotel work because I get to work in a nice place, wear a suit, and meet people. I enjoy making people feel comfortable and happy. I do not think I will own my own hotel. I would prefer to work for a big corporate chain of hotels. After I graduate, I am going to try to work in a U.S. hotel for a year. Then I am going to get a master's degree in hotel management. At some point in the future, I will go back to be near my family in Indonesia. I will probably work in Malaysia or Thailand because tourism is big business there. My dream job is to work at the Ritz Carlton in Bali!

Activity 5. Respond

Answer the questions about Endy's paragraph. Use complete sentences. The first one is done for you.

1. What is Endy interested in?

   <u>He is interested in business.</u>

2. What degree is he working on?

   _____

3. Why does he like hotel work?

   _____

4. What does Endy enjoy?

   _____

5. What does he <u>not</u> think he will do?

   _____

6. Where would Endy prefer to work?

   _____

7. What does Endy plan to do after he graduates?

   _____

8. Where will he probably work at some point in the future?

   _____

9. What is Endy's dream job?

   _____

Activity 6. Reading

Read Frank's ideas about his future work.

My Life as a Musician
by Frank Forke

When I was a little boy, my dream was to be a policeman. Then, at age nine, my parents gave me guitar lessons, and I decided to become a musician. That is still my goal. In three or four years, I will graduate with a bachelor's degree in music. Afterwards, I would like to teach and play guitar somewhere in Central or South America. Because I speak three languages, German, Spanish, and English, I hope to get a good job. I am going to try to teach at a music school with a good reputation and play at the best nightclubs. Money and fame do not interest me. I just want to have a reputation as a fine musician.

Activity 7. Respond

Answer the questions about Frank's paragraph. Use complete sentences. The first one is done for you.

1. What did Frank want to be when he was a little boy?

   He wanted to be a policeman.

2. What happened when Frank was nine years old?

   _____

3. What kind of degree does Frank hope to get?

   _____

4. Where would he like to go after he graduates?

   _____

5. Why does he hope to get a good job?

_____

6. What two things do <u>not</u> interest him?

_____

7. What is his final wish?

_____

 Grammar Activities

To write about the future, you will need to use the future tense in some of your verbs.

Future: Using *Will* + V

The future tense tells about a future event. The future tense is formed like this:

> *will* + V (no endings)

As you learned with *can* + V, the verb that follows does not have any endings and never changes from the base form. Look at these examples:

> I **will take** some science courses while I am working.
>
> Endy **will return** home one day.

Will is often contracted as *'ll* when subject pronouns are used, as in these examples:

I will take	=	*I'll take*
You will take	=	*You'll take*
He will take	=	*He'll take*
She will take	=	*She'll take*
It will take	=	*It'll take*
We will take	=	*We'll take*
They will take	=	*They'll take*

When the future tense verb is negative, the contraction is *won't*.

I will not take	=	*I won't take*

Activity 8. Using *Will* + V

Make the verb in parentheses into a future tense verb. The first one is done for you.

1. One day Ibrahim _____will take_____ (take) over his father's business.

2. In three or four years, Frank _____ (graduate) with a bachelor's degree in music.

3. Then he _____ (get) a good job.

4. Frank _____ (try) to teach at a music school with a good reputation.

5. One day Endy _____ (work) for a large corporate hotel chain.

6. He _____ (stay) in the U.S. and work a year as an intern.

7. At the end of his studies, Endy _____ (have) a master's degree in hotel management.

8. Someday he _____ (go) back to be near his family in Indonesia.

9. He _____ (work) in Malaysia or Thailand.

10. He _____ (try) to get a job at the Ritz Carlton in Bali!

Future: Using *Be Going To* + V

You may tell about the future in another way:

> *be going to* + V (no endings)

The meaning is almost the same as the future tense with *will*. The *be* verb will change with each subject pronoun. *Be* is always in present tense. Look at these examples:

> *I am going to take*
>
> *You are going to take*
>
> *He is going to take*
>
> *She is going to take*
>
> *It is going to take*
>
> *We are going to take*
>
> *They are going to take*

Activity 9. Using *Be Going To* + V

Change the future tense verbs in Activity 8 to a **be going to** + *V form. The first one is done for you.*

1. One day Ibrahim ____is going to take____ (take) over his father's business.

2. In three or four years, I _____ (graduate) with a bachelor degree in music.

3. In the future only college graduates _____ (be) able to get good jobs.

4. You _____ (try) to teach at a music school with a good reputation.

5. One day we _____ (work) for a large corporate hotel chain.

6. He _____ (stay) in the U.S. and work a year as an intern.

7. At the end of his studies, Endy _____ (have) a master's degree in hotel management.

8. Someday the students _____ (go) back to be near their families.

9. I _____ (work) in Malaysia or Thailand.

10. They _____ (try) to get jobs at the Ritz Carlton in Bali!

Writing Activities

Activity 10. Journal Topics

Are you ready to write just for fun? Write for 15 minutes without stopping on one of these topics. Try a new topic each day.

1. What kinds of jobs have you had in the past? Describe one that was difficult for you. Why was it difficult? Describe one that was easy for you. Why was it easy?

2. What kinds of work do your parents do? Can you see yourself doing the kind of work they do?

3. What kinds of work did your grandparents do? Can you see yourself doing that kind of work?

4. What kind of work does your best friend want to do? Would you like to do this type of work also? Discuss how this work will be (or won't be) good for your friend.

Activity 11. Guided Sentence Practice

Answer the questions in full sentences. Pay attention to all parts of the sentence, especially types of sentences.

1. What did you want to be when you were younger?_____

_____

2. What kind of career do you want now? _____

_____

3. If the two jobs are different, what changed your mind?_____

_____

4. What is your goal for the near future? _____

_____

5. What do you need to do to meet this goal?_____

_____

6. What is your goal for later in your career?_____

_____

7. Where would you like to work?_____

_____

8. How long do you wish to work? _____

_____

9. At the end of your working life, what would you like others to say about you? _____

_____

_____

Activity 12. Writing a First Draft

In the space provided or on a separate page, write a paragraph about a job you would like to do. Use the sentences you wrote in Activity 11 as a guide. Reread Endy's and Frank's paragraphs for ideas. Ibrahim's paragraph about his future work follows. You may like to use it as a guide too.

_____

_____

_____

_____

_____

_____

_____

_____

_____

_____

Sample Paragraph:

Selling Cars

by Ibrahim Aboumador

I love everything about cars. My ideal job is to work with cars. My parents own a used car lot. My father sold cars for many years at different car dealerships around town. This past year my parents had the opportunity to buy a car lot near our house. It was a scary decision for them. They used all their savings to start the business, but it is very successful so far. My father is a very honest person. He is like a good clothing sales clerk. He believes a car should fit a person like good clothes. I know they took this risk for me. One day I will take over the business. I thank my parents so much for this opportunity.

Sentence Variety

Variety is change. Sentence variety means different types of sentences within paragraphs. You have studied the different ways to write sentences. You now know about simple, compound, complex, and compound-complex sentences. In addition, you also know about how to add information to main subjects and verbs. You know about adjectives, prepositional phrases, renaming phrases, gerunds, and infinitives. Now that you know these ways to expand your sentences, use them! Sentence variety in a paragraph is important for good style and easy reading.

Keep these basic ideas in mind as you write:

- Try not to write all short, simple sentences.
- Combine short sentences into longer ones using compound, complex, and compound-complex sentences.
- Change your sentence beginnings—use dependent clauses, transitions, prepositional phrases, and renaming phrases to begin some sentences.
- Try writing a short sentence between two longer ones.
- In some sentences, separate the main subject and verb with words or phrases.
- Sometimes questions, exclamations, and commands can be a change from the usual S + V statement.

Activity 13. Identifying Sentences for Variety

Look at Frank's paragraph. Notice the different ways Frank varies his sentences. Look at the words in bold. Discuss with a partner how the words in bold follow the ideas of sentence variety.

Sample Paragraph:

When I was a little boy, my dream was to be a policeman. **Then, at age nine,** my parents gave me guitar lessons, **and I** decided to become a musician. **That is still my goal. In three or four years,** I will graduate with a bachelor's degree in music. **Afterwards,** I would like to teach and play guitar somewhere in Central or South America. **Because I speak three languages, German, Spanish, and English,** I hope to get a good job. I am going to try to teach at a music school with a good reputation and play at the best night clubs. **Money and fame do not interest me.** I just want to make a name for myself as a fine musician.

Revision

Activity 14. Peer Editing

Show your paragraph to two or three classmates. Ask them to answer the questions on the form. Your teacher will also read your paragraph.

Reader's Name _____

Writer's Name _____

1. What kind of future work does the writer want to do and why?

   _____

   _____

   _____

   _____

2. What special skills does the writer have for this type of work?

   _____

   _____

   _____

   _____

3. Does the author use any compound-complex sentences? Copy them here.

   _____

   _____

   _____

   _____

4. Where do you need or want more information? What can be added?

   _____

   _____

   _____

   _____

Activity 15. Writing Additional Drafts

Write a second draft of your paragraph on a separate sheet of paper. Use the ideas of your classmates and your teacher to write a better paragraph.

✔ Editing

It is time to check grammar. Remember to look for only one type of error at a time.

Activity 16. Working on Grammar

Look for mistakes in your paragraph. Check parts of sentences in this order:

- Look at **sentence structure.** How many simple sentences do you use? How many compound? How many complex? How many compound-complex? Are there any sentences that can be combined?

- Check **verbs.** Do you use the future tense when necessary? Check all forms.

- Check **sentence variety.** Are the beginnings of sentences different? Do you sometimes use beginning dependent clauses, transition words, or prepositional phrases? Are short sentences followed by longer sentences?

- Check for a clear **topic sentence, concluding sentence,** and good **detail.**

- Check for any **fragments.** Be sure **subjects and verbs agree.**

Activity 17. Preparing a Final Draft

When you feel sure that the grammar is as good as you can make it, hand in this last draft to your teacher. He or she may find more words that need to be changed. Make these changes. Then hand in a final draft.

Appendix A

Glossary of Basic Grammar Terms

adjective—a word that adds information to a noun. (See page 42.)

> Example: I saw a *blue* sky.

adverb—a word that adds information to verbs, adjectives, sentences, or other adverbs. (See page 15.)

> Example: The sky was *very* blue.

article—a word (either *a, an,* or *the*) that goes before the noun and adds information. (See page 130.)

> Example: *The* sky became dark with clouds.

clause—a group of words that has a subject and a verb. A clause may be independent or dependent. (See pages 19 and 51.)

> S + V
> Example: *I saw a blue sky.*

DCW—(dependent clause word or subordinating conjunction)—a word that makes clauses dependent to link with independent clauses. (See pages 51 and 68.)

> Example: *When* I looked up, I saw a blue sky.

dependent clause—a clause with a subject and a verb that must be linked with an independent clause and cannot stand alone as a sentence. (See page 51.)

> Example: *When I looked up,* I saw a blue sky.

gerund—a verb form (V*ing*) that acts like a noun in sentences. (See page 87.)

> S + V + Obj
> Example: I like *looking* at the sky.

independent clause—a complete sentence with at least one subject and one verb. Independent clauses can stand alone as a sentence. (See page 19.)

> Example: *I like looking at the sky.*

infinitive—a verb form (*to* + V) that acts like a noun in sentences. (See page 87.)

> Example: I like *to look* at the sky.

noun—a word for a person, place, thing, or feeling. (See page 8.)

> Example: I like looking at the *sky.*

object—a noun that tells who or what is receiving the action of the verb. (See page 26.)

Example: I saw a blue *sky*.

prepositional phrase—a phrase that contains at least a preposition and a noun. Sometimes there are other words that add information to the noun. (See page 76.)

Example: *In the sky*, there are clouds.

pronoun—a word that takes the place of a noun. There are subject and object pronouns. (See pages 8 and 27.)

Example: *I* saw a blue sky.

subject—a noun that tells who or what the sentence is about. (See page 8.)

Example: The *sky* is so very blue.

subordinating conjunction—see DCW.

transition—a word (or words) that links sentences to make a paragraph clearer. (See pages 15 and 47.)

Example: *At first*, I did not look at the sky much.

verb—a word that shows action or being. (See pages 9-10, 58-60, 73-75, 87, 102, 116-18.)

Example: The sky *is getting* dark now.

Appendix B

Punctuation Rules

Statements begin with a capital letter and end in a **period.**

> Example: Luke is a very good student.

Questions begin with a capital letter and end in a **question mark.**

> Example: Where does Luke study?

Exclamations begin with a capital letter and end in an **exclamation point.**

> Example: Luke really does study hard!

Commas are used to:

- **separate three or more words in a list** (See page 24.)

  > Example: This semester Luke is taking *English, math, and psychology.*

- **separate a compound sentence before the coordinating conjunction** *(and, but, or, so)* (See page 35.)

  > Example: Luke is a very good student, *and* he studies hard.

- **separate a dependent clause <u>before</u> an independent clause** (When the dependent clause comes after the independent clause, the comma is not necessary.) (See page 51.)

  > Example: *When he is not studying,* Luke works on campus.
  > Compare: Luke works on campus *when he is not studying.*

- **set off a renaming phrase** (See page 88.)

  > Example: Luke, *a student from Poland,* finds schools in the U.S. very different.

Appendix C

Spelling Rules

To form a V + *ing* (for progressive tenses and gerunds), follow these rules:

- To most verbs, simply add -*ing*.

  act → acting   check → checking

- To verbs ending in a consonant + -*e,* drop the -*e* and add -*ing*.

  smile → smiling   come → coming

- To verbs ending in one vowel + one consonant, double the consonant and add -*ing*.

  sit → sitting   get → getting

- In verbs of two syllables and ending in one vowel and one consonant, double the consonant only **if the stress is on the final syllable.**

  LISten → listening   preFER → preferring
  OPen → opening   adMIT → admitting

To form a V + -*ed* (for past tenses), follow these rules:

- To most verbs, simply add -*ed.*

  act → acted   check → checked

- To verbs ending in a consonant + -*e,* just add -*d.*

  smile → smiled   close → closed

- To verbs ending in one vowel + one consonant, double the consonant and add -*ed.*

  rob → robbed   stop → stopped

- To verbs ending in one consonant + -*y,* change the -*y* to -*i* and add -*ed.*

  reply → replied   marry → married

- In verbs of two syllables and ending in one vowel and one consonant, double the consonant only **if the stress is on the final syllable.**

  LISten → listened   preFER → preferred
  OPen → opened   adMIT → admitted

To form plural nouns, follow these rules:

- To most nouns, simply add *–s.*

  boy → boys   edge → edges

- To nouns ending in one consonant + *-y,* change the *-y* to *-i* and add *-es.*

  fly → flies   lady → ladies

- To nouns ending in an *-f* or *-fe,* change the *-f* or *-fe* to *-v* and add *-es.*

  wife → wives   leaf → leaves

- In nouns ending in *-sh, -ch, -ss,* or *-x,* add *-es.*

  wish → wishes   catch → catches

  class → classes   box → boxes

- In nouns ending in a consonant + *-o,* add *-es.*

  tomato → tomatoes   potato → potatoes

Appendix D

Count and Noncount Nouns

Remember this important information about **count nouns:**

- Count nouns can be *counted* and so can be plural.

  one *page,* two *pages,* three *pages*

- Singular count nouns must have a word in front of them: *a, an,* or *one.*

  a child   an animal   one boy

- Plural count nouns can stand alone without an article (zero article).

  Cars can be dangerous.
  Books are wonderful friends.

- Plural count nouns can also have quantity words in front of them.

  Some cars are safer than others.
  Many books are expensive.

Remember this important information about **noncount nouns:**

- Noncount nouns cannot be *counted* and so cannot be plural. Noncount nouns have one form only.

  help   furniture   advice

- Noncount nouns are considered singular and take singular verbs.

  The weather is very bad right now.

- Noncount nouns can stand alone without an article (zero article).

  Information can sometimes be hard to get.

- Noncount nouns can also have quantity words in front of them.

  A little money goes a long way.
  He has a lot of homework to do tonight.
  There is some furniture in the house.

Appendix E

Articles

Nouns can describe people, places, things, and feelings in three different ways. Articles are words that make these differences clear. These differences are called *references*.

General Reference

These nouns are described in a general way. They do not refer to anything specific. This reference is used to make general statements.

Singular Count Nouns *a, an* + singular count noun	Plural Count Nouns (zero article) + plural count noun	Noncount Nouns (zero article) + noncount noun
A book is always a good friend. (any book, all books)	*Books are always good friends.* (books in general)	*Homework can be dull.* (homework in general, not in particular)

Particular Reference

These nouns are no longer generalized. They exist as real objects, but they are not specified or identified. This reference is used to make a first mention.

Singular Count Nouns *a, an* + singular count noun	Plural Count Nouns quantity word + plural count noun	Noncount Nouns quantity word + noncount noun
I bought a book today. (one book, a real book, but we don't know what it is yet)	*There are some books over there for you to take home.* (real books that exist, not general)	*She has a lot of homework to do.* (not homework in the abstract but actual homework)

Specified Reference

These nouns exist and are specific and identified. The speakers (or writer and reader) both understand what they are. This reference is used to make a second mention.

Singular Count Nouns *the* + singular count noun	Plural Count Nouns *the* + plural count noun	Noncount Nouns *the* + noncount noun
The book that you gave me to read was very good. (a real book that we both know about)	*The books that you borrowed are on the table.* (real books we both know about)	*The students could not finish the homework.* (real homework known by speakers or reader and writer)

Appendix F

Verb Tense Summary

V = base form of the verb (the verb without any endings)

Simple Present Tense   *I, you, we, they* + V

he, she, it + V + *s*

Examples: Martin *plays* drums.

Martin and his roommate *play* music all the time.

Present Progressive Tense *I + am + Ving*

you, we, they + are + Ving

he, she, it + is + Ving

Examples: Martin *is playing* the drums now.

Martin and his roommate *are playing* in a band.

Simple Past Tense   *I, you, he, she, it, we, they* + *Ved*

Example: Martin *played* the drums in high school.

Past Progressive Tense   *I, he, she, it + was + Ving*

you, we, they + were + Ving

Examples: Martin *was playing* the drums last night.

Martin and his roommate *were playing* in a band last year.

Simple Future Tense   *I, you, he, she, it, we, they + will + V*

Example: Martin *will play* music for the rest of his life.

***Be Going to* Future Tense**   *I + am + going to + V*

you, we, they + are + going to + V

he, she, it + is + going to + V

Examples: Martin *is going to make* music for the rest of his life.

Martin and his roommate *are going to make* music all their lives.

Appendix G

Irregular Verbs

Base Form	Simple Past	Past Participle
be	was, were	been
become	became	become
begin	began	begun
break	broke	broken
bring	brought	brought
build	built	built
buy	bought	bought
catch	caught	caught
choose	chose	chosen
come	came	come
cost	cost	cost
cut	cut	cut
do	did	done
draw	drew	drawn
drink	drank	drunk
drive	drove	driven
eat	ate	eaten
fall	fell	fallen
feed	fed	fed
feel	felt	felt
fight	fought	fought
find	found	found
fly	flew	flown
forget	forgot	forgotten
get	got	gotten
give	gave	given
go	went	gone
grow	grew	grown
hang	hung	hung
have	had	had
hear	heard	heard
hit	hit	hit
hold	held	held
keep	kept	kept
know	knew	known
lay	laid	lain

Base Form	Simple Past	Past Participle
leave	left	left
lose	lost	lost
make	made	made
meet	met	met
pay	paid	paid
put	put	put
quit	quit	quit
read	read	read
ride	rode	ridden
run	ran	run
say	said	said
see	saw	seen
sell	sold	sold
send	sent	sent
shake	shook	shaken
sing	sang	sung
sit	sat	sat
sleep	slept	slept
speak	spoke	spoken
spend	spent	spent
stand	stood	stood
take	took	taken
teach	taught	taught
tell	told	told
think	thought	thought
throw	threw	thrown
understand	understood	understood
wear	wore	worn
win	won	won
write	wrote	written

Appendix H

Sentence Type Summary

Simple Sentence (Independent Clause)

S + V.

Example: Mesay lives with her parents.

Compound Sentence (2 Independent Clauses)

S + V,	*and* S + V.
	but
	or
	so

Example: Mesay lives with her parents, and she drives to school every day.

Complex Sentence (Dependent Clause + Independent Clause)

When + s + v	, S + V.
Before	
After	
Because	
Even though	

Example: Because she wants to save money, Mesay lives with her parents.

Complex Sentence (Independent Clause + Dependent Clause)

S + V +	*when* + s + v .
	before
	after
	because
	even though

Example: Mesay lives with her parents because she wants to save money.

Compound-Complex Sentence
(Independent Clause + Dependent Clause + Independent Clause)

S + V	+	*when* + s + v	, *and* + S + V.
		before	*but*
		after	*so*
		because	*or*
		even though	

<u>Example:</u> Mesay lives with her parents because she wants to save money, and she also likes being with her family.

Compound-Complex Sentence
(Dependent Clause + Independent Clause + Independent Clause)

When + s + v	, S + V	, + *and* + S + V.
Before		*but*
After		*so*
Because		*or*
Even though		

<u>Example:</u> Because she wants to save money, Mesay lives with her parents, and she also likes being with her family.

Answer Key

Chapter 1 (pages 1–17)

Activity 1 (page 2)

2. My (name) is Ana.
3. Does (she) (study) hard?
4. (Don't touch) that! ("You" is the implied subject.)
5. Where do the (students) (live)?
6. (Frank) (walks) to class every day.
7. (They) (eat) together every night.
8. (You) (look) so pretty!
9. (Is) her (son) 16 years old already?
10. Her (husband) (works) at the university too.

Activity 2 (page 3)

1. What is your name? What do you do?
2. Where are you from? How long have you been here? How do you like the U.S.?

Activity 3 (page 4)

Answers will vary.

Activity 4 (page 5)

Do is in front of the subject.

Activity 5 (page 6)

2. name, is
3. do, you
4. are, you
5. I, am
6. does, she
7. she, is
8. Do, they
9. they, like
10. do, they

Activity 7 (page 7)

2. He is from Venezuela.
3. He studies business administration.
4. He lives on campus in an apartment.
5. He thinks the apartment is small.
6. He likes being near his classes.
7. He likes the classes and the professors at the university.
8. They are helpful to the students.

Activity 8 (page 8)

2. She studies physics.
3. Does he study physics too?
4. They have two children!
5. We are good friends.
6. He studies music.
7. Does it have a good music program?
8. They are from a small town in Germany.
9. It is a peaceful place to live.
10. They can be exciting places to live.

Activity 9 (page 9)

2. are
3. am
4. is
5. are
6. has
7. have
8. have
9. has
10. have

Activity 10 (page 10)

2. walk
3. live
4. works
5. like
6. learns
7. comes
8. hate
9. study
10. enjoys

Activity 11 (page 11)

3. F— They live with their parents in an apartment near the university.
4. S
5. S
6. F—The youngest one, Andra, likes art and literature.
7. F—They are good in mathematics.
8. F—They make good grades in school.
9. S
10. S

Activities 12–18 (pages 13–17)

Answers will vary.

Chapter 2 (pages 18–33)

Activity 1 (page 20)

2. she, misses
3. mountains, are
4. people, come
5. people, ski

Activity 2 (page 21)

2. Leo and his family live in Salvador.
3. Two million people live and work in Salvador.
4. Many traditions and customs come from West African slaves.
5. Brazilian food and music are popular with the tourists.
6. Millions of people sing and dance in the streets during Carnival.

Activity 5 (page 23)

2. It is on the east coast of South Korea.
3. Mountains, lakes, and the ocean are all nearby.
4. They find friendly people and good seafood.
5. Winters are not too cold.
6. In the spring tourists hike in the mountains. In the summer they go to the beach. In the fall they go to see the lovely changing leaves. In the winter, there is skiing.
7. She misses her hometown.
8. She hopes to live there again one day.

Activity 6 (page 24)

1. Mountains, lakes, and the ocean are all nearby.
2. Visitors come and stay during all four seasons.

Activity 7 (page 24)

2. S—she, <u>wants</u>
3. S—Mesay, <u>comes</u>
4. S—name, <u>is</u>
5. P—she and her sister, <u>are</u>
6. S—Etsegenet, <u>is</u>
7. P—Mesay and Etsegenet, <u>study</u>
8. P—They, <u>have</u>
9. P—Samson and Kidus, <u>are</u>
10. P—Mesay, Samson, and Kidus, <u>live</u>

Activity 8 (page 25)

2. has
3. are
4. come
5. hike

Activity 9 (page 26)

2. are
3. is
4. are
5. are

Activity 10 (page 27)

2. Salvadoran cooks use peanuts, coconut, and okra to make some of our delicious dishes.
3. Our music and dance also have roots in Africa.
   Slaves in the field would dance and fight.
   Many visitors also come to Salvador for the music and dance of Carnival in the spring.

Activities 11–13 (pages 28–30)

Answers will vary.

Activity 14 (page 31)

2. African slaves: sentences 3, 4, 6, 8, and 11

3. heritage and culture: sentences 4, 5, and 14

4. music and dance: sentences 8, 9, 10, 12, and 13

Activities 15–18 (pages 32–33)

Answers will vary

Chapter 3 (pages 34–49)

Activity 1 (page 36)

2. The house is in a quiet neighborhood, and it is convenient to shopping and schools.

3. I study in my room, or I work at the computer in the den.

4. The kitchen is next to the dining room, so we can eat most of our meals at the dining room table.

5. My bedroom has a good view of the backyard, and I love looking at the pretty garden. OR
My bedroom has a good view of the backyard, so I love looking at the pretty garden.

6. We spend family time in the living room listening to music, or we watch TV in the den.

7. My parents sleep in one bedroom with a door leading to a bathroom, but there is another bedroom with an attached bathroom in it. OR
My parents sleep in one bedroom with a door leading to a bathroom, and there is another bedroom with an attached bathroom in it.

8. I am the oldest child, so I have the other bedroom and bath.

9. My parents want to sleep close to my little brothers, so they sleep in the upstairs bedroom next to their rooms.

10. I sleep downstairs next to the kitchen, but I do not go there late at night for snacks!

Activity 2 (page 37)

3. S

4. C

5. S

6. S

7. C

8. C

9. C

10. S

Activity 3 (page 38)

2. masterpiece

3. three-dimensional

4. software

5. design

6. texture

7. model

8. fascinated

9. process

10. skeleton

Activity 5 (page 39)

2. 3-D design seems a little like creating a sculpture.

3. It is better because the computer can fix mistakes fast.

4. He begins with a simple shape and tries to model it into something else.

5. This process can take many hours.

6. He needs to add color, texture, and light.

7. Light is the hardest to add.

8. Light on the computer does not act like natural light.

9. Movies like *Shrek* and *Ice Age* are masterpieces of 3-D design.

Activity 6 (page 41)

2. In German universities students do not (don't) take classes only in their special fields of study.

3. It is not (isn't) strange for me to take courses from other academic fields.

4. My friend is not (isn't) in an Asian literature class.

5. These classes do not (don't) interest me.

6. They are not (aren't) so different from her music major.

7. One thing about the university does not (doesn't) shock me.

8. Some students do not (don't) eat and drink in class.

9. They do not (don't) put their feet on the desk in front of them sometimes.

10. Students in Germany do not (don't) show more respect.

Activity 7 (page 42)

2. Sometimes I (am) bored with the freshman courses.

3. These courses (are) necessary.

4. Many college students (are not) prepared.

5. Some high schools (are) sometimes (not) very strong.

6. The professors in the university (are) very friendly.

7. Their attitude (is) very helpful.

8. In Poland, the professors (are) sometimes unfriendly.

9. In Poland, only lectures, homework, and tests (are) important.

10. In the U.S. the connection between life and learning (is) good.

Activities 8–15 (pages 43–49)

Answers will vary.

Chapter 4 (pages 50–66)

Activity 1 (page 52)

3. Before Endy decided to study in the U.S., he thought about it for many months.

4. His mother cried when he left.

5. After Mesay finished her homework, she watched television for a few minutes.

6. Mesay went for a walk before she ate dinner last night.

7. When her father got a job in the U.S., the family applied for visas.

8. After her sister moved into an apartment, the house was quiet.

9. Martin was ten when his mother died.

10. Before Martin left Bolivia, he said good-bye to all his family members.

Activity 2 (page 53)

2. j

3. c

4. a

5. f

6. b

7. h

8. k

9. e

10. g

11. d

Activity 3 (page 54)

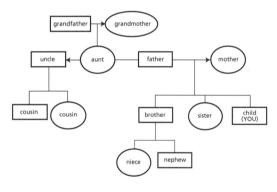

Activity 5 (page 55)

2. Martin has the smallest family. There are Martin and his two brothers.

3. Mesay is the oldest child in her family.

4. Martin and Endy are the youngest in their families.

5. Martin and Endy lost their parents.

6. Martin was ten when his mother died. He was twenty when his father died. Endy was seventeen when his father died.

7. Endy and Mesay still live with family.

8. Martin does not live with family.

9. Martin and Endy have nieces and nephews.

Activity 6 (page 57)

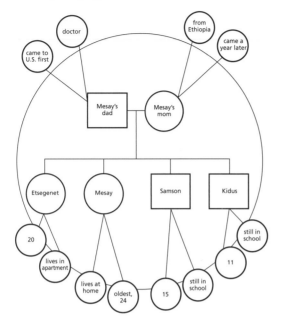

Activity 7 (page 58)

2. lived
3. died
4. passed
5. asked
6. wanted

Activity 8 (page 59)

2. knew
3. made
4. said
5. felt
6. forgot
7. spoke
8. understood
9. left
10. saw

Activity 9 (page 60)

2. Did you take the test already?
3. What did you say to the teacher?
4. Yesterday the child wanted a glass of milk.
5. His brother did not feel happy.

Activities 10–16 (pages 61–66)

Answers will vary.

Chapter 5 (pages 67–82)

Activity 1 (page 69)

3. Because my sister and mother had only two months to plan the wedding, they had to work fast.
4. Because my mother loves my sister very much, she worked very hard.
5. Even though they didn't have much time, everything worked out.
6. Because our parents are from Egypt, Sheri wanted a Middle Eastern wedding.
7. Sheri's husband wanted one too because his family is Moroccan.
8. They served typical food from our countries even though Middle Eastern cooks are hard to find.
9. Sheri wore a traditional wedding dress because her mother-in-law brought her one from Morocco.
10. Because they worked so hard, it was a day to remember!

Activity 2 (page 70)

2. independent
3. comfortable
4. ugly
5. happy
6. hate
7. play
8. maid
9. park

Activity 4 (page 71)

2. When she was growing up, her parents sheltered her completely.
3. She didn't like it at all because she was so homesick.
4. When the weather turned colder, she needed to buy a pair of warm boots.
5. She went shopping, but she didn't know what to buy.
6. She bought nothing.

7. She was happy, but she was also ashamed.

8. Her sister teases her.

9. She asks, "Do you need a new pair of boots?"

Activity 6 (page 72)

Answers will vary.

Activity 7 (page 74)

2. were

3. celebrated

4. started

5. did not realize

6. looked

7. were shaking

8. were having

9. was

10. were

11. went

12. tried

13. stopped

14. was

Activity 8 (page 75)

3. Then later she said that she didn't want to go.

4. Another day Benito said that he wanted to take her to a movie.

5. Irma said that she would love to go.

6. On the day of the date she said that she was bringing a friend with her.

7. Benito said that the movie would be enjoyable for them all.

8. After the movie he said that he would like to go get ice cream.

9. The friend said that she needed to go home.

10. Irma said that she would like to stay and have some ice cream.

11. At the ice cream shop Irma said (to him) that she liked him.

Activity 9 (page 77)

2. We did a lot of work.

3. We did it in two short months.

4. Mom found a ballroom near our house.

5. We ordered food from a caterer.

6. We made arrangements for relatives.

7. They came from Egypt.

8. They also came from Morocco.

Activities 10–17 (pages 78–82)

Answers will vary.

Chapter 6 (pages 83–94)

Activity 1 (page 84)

<u>Note:</u> *That* can be left out of the following sentences.

2. I know (that) he is still very young.

3. I believe (that) he was still a teenager when he turned professional.

4. I think (that) he started his career as a shortstop.

5. I believe (that) he plays left field now.

6. I think (that) he has a very good arm.

7. I know (that) he can throw the ball hard.

8. I believe (that) he is a good batter too.

9. I believe (that) he is the youngest player to have the most home runs in major league baseball.

10. I think (that) Miguel Cabrera is at the start of a very successful career.

Activity 2 (page 85)

1. e

2. b

3. g

4. d

5. a

6. h

7. i

8. c

9. j

10. f

Activity 4 (page 86)

2. She offered to teach conversational English every day during lunch.

3. He thought she was dedicated to give up lunch.

4. She knew that English would help them get scholarships and find jobs.

5. He was shocked.

6. He could not understand very many words in English.

7. She used only English when she knew they knew the words.

8. She made the classes interesting with songs and fun stories.

9. She encouraged them to bring in the English they found in their daily lives.

10. He feels very grateful to his teacher.

Activity 5 (page 88)

2. watching

3. to work

4. eating/to eat

5. to work

6. to teach

7. to get

8. studying/to study

9. being/to be

10. working

Activity 6 (page 89)

2. a terrible sickness

3. a long time

4. a kind person

5. a difficult job for her

6. a hard worker

7. a gift from her to her friends

8. ten thousand dollars

Activities 7–14 (pages 90–94)

Answers will vary.

Chapter 7 (pages 95–109)

Activity 1 (page 96)

2. She was a woman who knew how to live.

3. She married a man who was a colonel in the Air Force.

4. After World War II, they moved to a German city that was very poor.

5. She organized a club that helped poor German girls.

6. She also moved to Japan with her husband who was stationed there.

7. Aunt Virginia started a school for Japanese women who wanted to learn English.

8. Aunt Virginia told exciting stories that made my husband want to travel to the Orient.

9. She loved to read books that were full of adventure.

10. She loved visiting places that were far away.

Activity 2 (page 97)

2. She gave wonderful parties, which were quite large.
   She gave wonderful parties that were quite large.

3. She hired musicians who were the best in the city.
   She hired musicians that were the best in the city.

4. She served food that was delicious.
   She served food, which was delicious.

5. Sometimes she invited us to small dinners that were for family only.
   Sometimes she invited us to small dinners, which were for family only.

6. At the age of 83, her husband had a stroke that left him very weak.
   At the age of 83, her husband had a stroke, which left him very weak.

7. For nine years Aunt Virginia cared for him in their house that became like a hospital.

8. She nursed her husband with a love that was patient and kind.

9. She died soon after her husband with a peace that was beautiful.

10. I will always admire this woman who changed my life.

Activity 3 (page 98)

2. opportunity

3. attitude

4. challenge

5. encourage

6. adore

7. inspire

8. advice

9. overcome

10. strict

Activity 4 (page 99)

1. s = who, v = works; S = coworker, V = is

2. s = that, v = can make; S = opportunity, V = is

3. s = that, v = shows; S = attitude, V = is

4. s = that, v = is; S = challenge, V = is

5. s = that, v = helps; S = to encourage, V = is

6. s = that, v = is; S = to adore, V = is

7. s = that, v = makes; S = to inspire, V = is

8. s = that, v = can help; S = advice, V = is

9. s = situation, v = cannot continue; S = to feel overcome, V = is

10. s = who, v = is; S = person, V = wants

Activity 6 (page 100)

2. Mary decided to go back to school to get a degree in music.

3. Mary has children and grandchildren to keep her busy.

4. Mary wanted a challenge in her life.

5. She is at school every day at 8 o'clock doing homework. She has bad knees but

never minds walking up the stairs. She looks at problems as opportunities.

6. She gives him good advice.

7. Sometimes he helps her with her computer.

Activity 8 (page 101)

2. Coworkers, friends, and neighbors all respected him.

3. When Shahzad was a young child, his grandfather taught him right from wrong. He taught him the proper way to speak and how to behave.

4. He encouraged Shahzad to work in school for the highest grades.

5. He taught him to go to sleep early at night and get up early in the morning.

6. He started making excellent grades.

7. In college he still plans his time in this way.

Activity 9 (page 103)

2. to be

3. to help

4. to thank

5. love

6. to earn

7. go

8. complain

9. to study

10. to be

Activities 10–17 (pages 103–109)

Answers will vary.

Chapter 8 (pages 110–23)

Activity 1 (page 111)

2. His grandfather passed away when Shahzad was in high school, but his dream is still alive.

3. Even though Shahzad was always good in math and biology, he did not have a high enough score to get into medical school in

Pakistan, so his father encouraged him to study computer science.

4. When his father left for the U.S., he asked Shahzad to come with him, and Shahzad said he would think about it.

5. Even though Shahzad did not want to leave Pakistan at that time, he knew it would be a good opportunity, and he would get a good job.

6. Now Shahzad is working on a degree in computer science, but he cannot stop thinking that he could still be a doctor.

7. Because he still wants to help people get well, he thinks that computer work will soon bore him.

8. After he works a few years, he will take a few science courses, and he can apply to medical school in the U.S.

Activity 2 (page 113)

A job is regular work that someone is paid to do.

Work is physical or mental effort toward a result, like a job.

A career is the progress of work someone does throughout his or her life.

A profession is work that requires special training or skill.

An occupation is a formal way of saying what a person does to earn a living.

Employment is paid work in a company or organization.

Activity 3 (page 113)

2. decision
3. ideal
4. management
5. prefer
6. comfortable
7. intern
8. corporate chain
9. reputation

Activity 5 (page 114)

2. He is working on a degree in hotel, restaurant, and tourism management.

3. He likes hotel work because he gets to work in a nice place, wear a suit, and meet people.

4. He enjoys making people feel comfortable and happy.

5. He does not think he will own his own hotel.

6. Endy would prefer to work for a big corporate chain of hotels.

7. He is going to try to work in a U.S. hotel for a year.

8. He will probably work in Malaysia or Thailand.

9. His dream job is to work at the Ritz Carlton in Bali.

Activity 7 (page 115)

2. His parents gave him guitar lessons, and he decided to become a musician.

3. He hopes to graduate with a degree in music.

4. He would like to teach and play guitar in Central or South America.

5. He hopes to get a good job because he speaks three languages.

6. Money and fame do not interest him.

7. He wants to have a reputation as a fine musician.

Activity 8 (page 117)

2. will graduate
3. will get
4. will try
5. will work
6. will stay
7. will have
8. will go
9. will work
10. will try

Activity 9 (page 118)

2. am going to graduate

3. are going to be able

4. are going to try

5. are going to work

6. is going to stay

7. is going to have

8. are going to go

9. am going to work

10. are going to try

Activities 10–17 (pages 118–23)

Answers will vary.